The United States

vs.

Santa Claus

How the U.S. Government Destroyed Christmas

by

Brian Sack and Jack Helmuth

LONDON   NEW YORK   TORONTO   SYDNEY

To Antek, Eden, Jack IV and Stasiu, from Santa.

DISCLAIMER

We have been asked by our legal department to write a disclaimer stating that this book is a work of fiction, parody and satire. The newspaper headlines you see existed only in our imaginations. The stories are total fabrications. All of the emails contained in the work are the products of authors' imagination and were not written by any of the people to whom they are attributed. Every page is all conjecture and exaggeration and bull-hooey, solely for the purpose of entertainment.

Except for all the parts that aren't!*

Death to legal departments!

—*Brian Sack & Jack Helmuth*

---

* Disclaimer: There are no parts that are real. That was a joke that our lawyers wanted us to state is a joke. Lawyers don't have good senses of humor

AUTHOR'S NOTE

December 13, 2044

As a father, there are certain questions that you dread your child asking you.

Q: Why do people hurt each other?
A: *I don't know, sweetie. Some people are just bad.*

Q: Where do babies come from?
A: *Ask your mother.*

Q: Can boys get married to boys?
A: *Good lord, when is your mother getting home?*

Q: What is Christmas, Daddy?
A: *[leaves room]*

I wasn't prepared for my seven-year-old to ask the Christmas question. I had begun to wonder if my son would ever even hear about Christmas, but I guess playground rumors* persist even in this age of telepathic messaging.

I closed the door so that his brother wouldn't be able to hear us talk. "Where did you hear that, buddy?" I asked. "Did one of your teachers tell you about that in school?" I was trying to sound as casual as possible.

---

* Rumors mostly persist during "Recessercise," a little-known provision of ObamaCare that began back in 2017. It was a mandated $4 billion youth exercise program that required "children to exercise in non-competitive ways." The "non-competitive" portion of that started in 2015 after the Hurt Feelings Act made labeling children "winners" or "losers" illegal, unless you were labeling everyone a "winner."

"Well, it was after the Pledge of Allegiance* and I was walking to my first class—"

"Oh, what class?" I asked, hoping to distract him from this whole Christmas business.

"History."

"Fun! I used to write history books before the U.S. Department of History Books took over. What did you learn in history?"

"About Christopher Columbus being a mass murderer."

"Oh brother."

"Anyway, Daddy, I heard my friends talking about it. What is Christmas?"

I paused for a long time, trying to figure out how to explain it—or if I should even try. Perhaps a white lie was in order. After all, my father had lied to me about where babies came from— and I'd turned out fine. (It was only when I was twenty-two that I finally realized there was no such place as "The Boy Store.")

But now, as I looked into my son's eyes, I resolved to tell him the truth, although I knew it wouldn't be easy. For starters, I barely even remembered Christmas myself, as I was just a year or two older than what my son is now when it all just . . . stopped. I don't remember a lot of the details, but I do remember the feeling that I used to have during that wonderful time of year: joyous and innocent; festive and communal. It was the joy of giving just as much as it was the joy of receiving.

It was, in a word, *beautiful.*

Then it was gone. I remember how disappointed I was that first December after Christmas was changed to "Holiday," and I'll never forget the gift the government sent me that year. It was my first Holiday present and the first of what would be many years of disappointment.

---

* The words of the Pledge of Allegiance were changed in 2021 to "I pledge allegiance, to the President, of the United States of America. And to the Republic, for which he/she/or it stands, because we don't see gender. One nation, under sky, indivisible, with liberty and justice for all. Guns are bad."

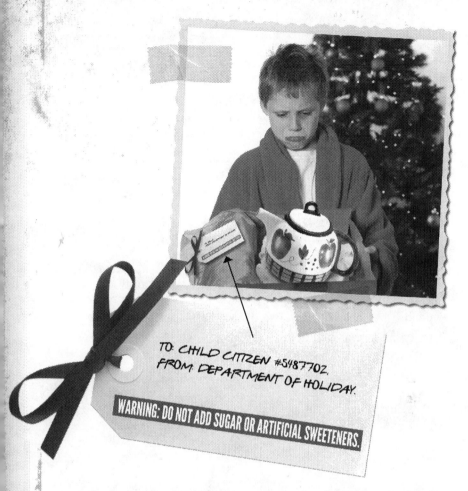

TO: CHILD CITIZEN #5487702.
FROM: DEPARTMENT OF HOLIDAY.

WARNING: DO NOT ADD SUGAR OR ARTIFICIAL SWEETENERS.

As I sat there looking at my son, a flood of feelings washed over me: sadness for having one of the most special and magical elements of childhood taken away from me, and anger over the fact that my children would never experience that feeling at all. The magic of Christmas was gone. Forever.

"Sit down," I said, "and I'll tell you everything I remember."

For the next three hours my son sat on my lap and I told him about Santa and the trees and lights and presents and stockings; the cookies and milk, the reindeer and elves, the carols and all the other traditions. I told him about the origins of the holiday, and I sang songs to him that I didn't even know I remembered.

That's when I decided to write this book—the first non-government-authorized history book written in years—to let Americans know the real story of what happened to Santa Claus. It will be jarring to read a book in this style, as everything you'll read is true and objective.* When it comes to the modern history of Christmas, "The Truth Lives Here."**

Thanks to the prevalence of whistle-blowers, the fastest (and, in fact, *only*) area of American job growth, I have been able to put this book together with a mixture of previously highly classified documents (never before seen by the American public) as well as archival footage such as newspaper clippings and official transcripts.

It is up to you to share this book with others and keep the memory and spirit of Christmas alive. Back in 2013, self-publishing meant that you probably weren't a good enough writer to get a book deal. In 2044 it means something completely different. It means you're fighting back.

When I was a kid, the question that parents dreaded most wasn't being asked about Christmas; it was being asked, "Is Santa Claus real?"

As it turns out, the answer was "yes." He was real. Christmas was real. And boy do I miss it.

—BY ANONYMOUS

---

* An old word that used to mean "not influenced by personal feelings or opinions in considering and representing facts."

** The slogan of Glenn Beck's former website TheBlaze, which went bankrupt after Mr. Beck spent hundreds of millions of dollars to project his face on the actual moon for what he deemed "a revolution in entertainment," but which, in fact, scared billions of people across the globe.

CONTENTS

Author's Note iii

Cast of Characters. ix

1. For Whom the Bell Jingles 2

2. Yes, Hank Johnson, There Is a Santa Claus . . . 16

3. Something's Rotten in the State of Nanny 32

4. Santa the Poor Role Model 48

5. Santa the Tax Evader 62

6. Santa the Polluter .76

7. Santa the Animal Abuser 90

8. Santa the Defendant 104

9. Santa the Taskmaster 118

10. Santa the Arms Peddler 138

11. Santa the Saboteur 152

12. Santa the Spy 166

13. As the Tide Turns 176

14. The *Titanic* 186

15. Setting Their Sights on Santa 194

Epilogue 204

Fun Santa Facts #1 212

Fun Santa Facts #2 216

Acknowledgments 222

CAST OF CHARACTERS

BAUCUS, MAX United States senator from Montana who didn't spend a lot of time in Montana. Served from 1978 to 2015. Considered a moderate Democrat by many. Three marriages, but only one child (whom he named "Zeno" for reasons we'll never fully understand).

BECK, GLENN Talk show host, author, and entertainer. Amassed the world's largest collection of patriotic handkerchiefs. Died of dehydration in 2021 after crying over his "love for America" for six straight days.

BIDEN, JOE Vice president of the United States under Barack Obama. Biden ran a failed bid for the presidency in 2020 and managed to accidentally offend almost all minorities except gay albinos. Biden's Secret Service code name was "Dumbass."

BLOOMBERG, MICHAEL Mayor of New York City from 2001 to 2013. Beloved for his ability to know what was right for every individual and make decisions on their behalf. The famous Statue of Bloomberg now stands in New York Harbor, telling boaters to slow down.

BO The First Dog, or DOTUS. A black and white Portuguese water dog (though considered just black by the media). Went on to star in Will Smith's remake of *Benji*, with Bo playing a kidnapper and Jaden Smith playing the role of Benji.

CLAUS, SANTA A revered figurehead for the once-popular "Christmas" holiday. His kindheartedness and generous nature endeared him to children of all ages. His ability to fit his large frame down small chimneys baffled physicists.

CLINTON, HILLARY Former secretary of state and first female president of the United States. Won the election handily after the GOP decided to nominate Mitt Romney a second time "just to see what would happen." Freaks out if you say "Benghazi!" within earshot.

CLINTON, WILLIAM JEFFERSON The forty-second president of the United States, who touched the lives and breasts of many Americans during and after his presidency. Freaks out if you say "Your wife's coming!" within earshot.

CLOONEY, GEORGE Famous actor whose dashing good looks and charm endeared him to millions. Died in 2037. Named *People* magazine's Sexiest Man Not Alive in 2038.

CNN Television network best known for covering the O. J. Simpson Slow-Mo Car Chase in 1994. After struggling to regain audience share it was purchased in 2015 by Kim Kardashian and Kanye West to facilitate a twenty-four-hour broadcast of their children's every waking moment.

CRAIGSLIST The Internet equivalent of newspaper classifieds that facilitates the purchase and sale of cars and antiques and also allows very unattractive people to falsely advertise themselves as "sexy" and "good-looking."

FACEBOOK A multibillion-dollar enterprise that allows individuals to post pictures of what they're eating for lunch.

FOX NEWS See MSNBC.

HITLER, ADOLF A real psychopants sourpuss who rained on everyone's parade, murdered millions, and started a global conflagration that got millions more killed. Now synonymous with anyone you don't like.

HOLDER, ERIC Former attorney general under the Obama administration whose ability to withstand repeated scandals was legendary. No one has ever seen Mr. Holder and Oprah Winfrey's "partner," Stedman Graham, in the same room together.

HUFFINGTON POST An Internet newspaper created by millionaire Arianna Huffington, who then sold it to AOL for millions of dollars. Its content was provided by journalists who primarily worked for free, penning countless articles lambasting corporations and unfairness.

INTERNAL REVENUE SERVICE The federal agency tasked with the collection of taxes. Also privately tasked with harassing conservative organizations and individuals deemed troublesome by the sitting president.

JOHNSON, HANK United States congressman from Georgia known for his intellectual capacity and eloquence. Tireless advocate for the rights of helium as a gas and wholly determined to prevent islands from capsizing.

LEW, JACK Secretary of the Treasury, known for having a signature that looked like the kind of halfhearted scribble you leave on those electronic signature pads at the supermarket.

MADDOW, RACHEL A regrettably hair-styled and intelligent host of an eponymous television program on the MSNBC network. Threw herself out a twelve-story window after being asked to cohost with Al Sharpton but screamed, "It's not racism!" all the way down.

McDONOUGH, DENIS White House chief of staff under the Obama administration. Famously insecure about the spelling of his first name, as were his ten siblings: Nuttocks, Ragina, Mesticles, Foobies, Oss, Enus, Sutthead, Wouchebag, Gildo, and Litties.

MICHAELS, DAVID As assistant secretary of labor for the Occupational Safety and Health Administration, Michaels was in charge of picking the font that goes on the OSHA workplace posters that no one reads.

MORGAN, PIERS Successor to the legendary Larry King and host of the not particularly popular *Piers Morgan Tonight* program on CNN. Morgan came to the United States as part of a work exchange program with the BBC. Once in the country, his visa was revoked by Great Britain under the "He's Your Problem Now Act."

MSNBC A trusted source of news for individuals willing to sacrifice journalistic integrity for the preferred benefit of having their viewpoints reinforced by an openly partisan punditry.

NATIONAL SECURITY AGENCY Highly secretive spy agency that specialized in intercepting overseas transmissions until they got spooked by a scary Islamist who lived in a cave. Now specializes in intercepting everything, everywhere at the expense of the Bill of Rights and stuff.

NEW YORK POST One of the largest-circulation newspapers in the country. Famous for classy "pun" headlines and using shorter words that are easier to read and pronounce. The only newspaper a genuinely illiterate person can read and comprehend.

NEW YORK TIMES One of the most influential newspapers in the world, called "the paper of record." People who read it strongly believe they are better than you.

OBAMA, BARACK HUSSEIN The forty-fourth president of the United States, who triumphed over the McCain/Palin ticket due in large part to a savvy marketing campaign centered around the slogan "Yes We Can." Following the election the slogan was changed to "What Do We Do Now?"

OBAMA, MICHELLE The First Lady of the United States, or FLOTUS. Presumptive pants-wearer in the Obama household. Set out to tackle childhood obesity by nagging everyone to death about it—also known as the Bloomberg Method.

OCCUPATIONAL SAFETY AND HEALTH ADMINISTRATION Federal organization tasked with printing word-filled posters in both English and Spanish, which are required to be mounted in all company break rooms in a place where they can easily be ignored.

PELOSI, NANCY Former Speaker of the United States House of Representatives. One of the wealthiest members of Congress, which is weird because Democrats traditionally hate rich people. Her chilling stare was used to refreeze parts of the Arctic Circle that had deteriorated due to climate change.

PEREZ, THOMAS Former United States secretary of labor who once got a jelly-of-the-month membership as a gift from Marco Rubio in Rubio's attempt to suck up to every Hispanic in America.

REID, HARRY Nevada senator and former Senate majority leader. In 2018 Reid was found guilty of illegally using campaign funds to purchase the Excalibur casino in Las Vegas (which he renamed to Harrycalibur Reidcalibur). Everyone hates him.

ROOSEVELT, FRANKLIN DELANO The thirty-second president of the United States. Architect of "The Really, Incredibly Expensive Idea," which was later renamed to the shorter and more palatable "New Deal." Credited with building New York's Taconic Parkway so that he could get to his estate in Hyde Park more quickly.

RUDOLPH THE RED-NOSED REINDEER Had a very shiny nose, and if you ever saw it you would even say it glows. In Will Smith's remake of *Rudolph* he was played by Jaden Smith.

SCHULTZ, DEBBIE WASSERMAN Shock-haired congresswoman from Florida and chair of the Democratic National Committee from 2011 to 2016. Subject of a conspiracy theory posited by Alex Jones that suggested she was actually a robot designed solely to deliver talking points in a shrill, aggravating voice. It was the only thing Alex Jones ever got right.

SCHUMER, CHARLES Possessed the uncanny ability to sniff out a television camera or radio microphone from distances as great as five miles. New York senator, 1999–2017. Total dick, 1950–current.

THE BLAZE Famous gay rights newsletter founded in the Castro district of San Francisco in 1979. Also a former monthly magazine for retired firefighters. Also a news network and website with the tagline "The Truth Lives Here," which was changed in 2015 to "Don't Judge Us by the Comment Section."

UNITED STATES SECRET SERVICE A federal law enforcement agency tasked with protecting various important members of the government and coming up with cool nicknames for them. Fun to party with.

USA TODAY Newspaper famous for being television in print form. Pioneered the use of pretty colors and charts in order to convey simple thoughts and ideas to a readership that could only read in pictures. Sold in 2016 to *Us Weekly*. If you learn something from reading either publication then something is wrong with you.

WASHINGTON POST Famous for breaking Woodward and Bernstein's Watergate story, which felled Nixon. Now the country's foremost employer of men and women who graduated from college with degrees in Native American feminism and Tibetan healing chants.

WERFEL, DANIEL Served as principal deputy commissioner of the Internal Revenue Service before becoming acting commissioner of the Internal Revenue Service and then King Overlord Merciless Persecutor of the Internal Revenue Service. That title was phased out and replaced by Acting Tax Guy. Pioneered changing IRS red flags to purple flags because they are considered to be less aggressive.

The United States

vs.

Santa Claus

1.

FOR WHOM THE
BELL JINGLES

odern-day folks who hear about "The War on Christmas" usually think about the actual war. But when I was a child, the "War on Christmas" was "fought" by overly sensitive local politicians who would throw a fit if someone said "Merry Christmas" to a rabbi, and in turn take a bulldozer to the manger on the town square to make up for the offense. Looking back on it now, I feel a great sense of nostalgia for the days when an atheist would scream about how Christian this Christian holiday was.

The sad fact is, the name "Santa Claus" has been dragged through the mud now for so long that it's developed into a swear word. In fact, no hip-hop album released in recent memory has shied away from using the name in a derogatory way.* It even turned into a verb, with "Santa-Clausing" (spray-painting homeless people red and white) becoming popular among some youths.

It might be hard to believe now, but back in 2013 Santa Claus was an absolutely revered figure in the United States. Most polls showed his approval rating at 100 percent. That's right: Everyone, regardless of their religion, race, or creed, loved Santa Claus like crazy. Even gangstas who couldn't count letters.

---

* Every song on Kanye West's nineteenth album, *Pfffft*, contained the "SC-word."

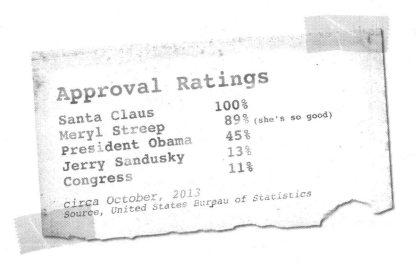

Approval Ratings

Santa Claus	100%
Meryl Streep	89% (she's so good)
President Obama	45%
Jerry Sandusky	13%
Congress	11%

circa October, 2013
Source, United States Bureau of Statistics

By 2015, when the case against Santa reached its feverish peak, those approvals were down to nearly 20 percent. That is a loss of nearly 150 percent.* How did this tremendous decline in support for Mr. Claus happen? That is what this book is contractually obligated to document for the next 45,326 words.

The United States government first learned that Santa Claus was real in 1942—this despite the famous 1897 editorial "Yes Virginia, There Is a Santa Claus," which various government officials had written off as "codswallop."**

The "realness" of Santa had been questioned for as long as the realness of Bigfoot (real), the Loch Ness Monster (not real), and the female orgasm (still undetermined—but currently the subject of a clandestine $13 million government study at Stanford University's William Jefferson Clinton School of Hotties). But it wasn't until a top-secret White House encounter that Uncle Sam (ironically, not real) learned just how real Santa really was.

President Franklin D. Roosevelt (of dime fame) was out for a wheel in the Rose Garden on the evening of December 23, 1942, when, according to secret White House transcripts released under the Freedom of Informa-

---

* I "graduated" from public high school. Please don't ask why I put "graduated" in quotes.
** Every song on Kenneth Pemberton's 1902 album, *By Jove!*, contained the word *codswallop*.

tion Act, Santa Claus suddenly appeared. He had been moved to meet the president after reading his heartfelt letter that had appeared at his workshop days prior. Santa was so taken by Roosevelt's innocence and charm that he showed up on the day before his busiest day of the year to answer the letter in person. Here is the transcript of that meeting, released now to the American public for the first time ever.

FILED
DUPLICATE
DEC 2 0 1944

White House Transcript: December 23, 1942

PRESIDENT ROOSEVELT: My prayers have been answered. You are real!

SANTA: Of course I'm real. Just like Bigfoot.

PRESIDENT ROOSEVELT: What about the female or—

Santa: Santa doesn't know! And Santa doesn't talk about such things. Come on. Jeez.

PRESIDENT ROOSEVELT: Of course. I'm sorry. I wrote you because this is the time when good men of all kinds must band together and fight evil.

SANTA: Yours was a very special letter to Santa, Frankie. It truly moved me.

PRESIDENT ROOSEVELT: You must think it's ridiculous that a world leader wrote Santa Claus with a wish list.

SANTA: Not at all. In fact, many of the participants in this horrible war have contacted me. Churchill asked for peace on the European continent. Stalin sent me a strange letter stating that he didn't believe in me, asked for a million troops for the front lines, and said that I had one week to comply or he would "purge" me. Ho ho ho—my God is that guy nuts.

PRESIDENT ROOSEVELT: Wow. Can you do that? That thing about the troops?

SANTA: Make people? Only if Mrs. Claus has had one too many eggnogs. Otherwise, no, there's no magic that can make human beings.

PRESIDENT ROOSEVELT: How did Stalin take that?

SANTA: Not well. I gave him a bunch of toys to distribute to his people like a good socialist should. I bet he kept them all, though. He's kind of a Communist Party–pooper, isn't he?

PRESIDENT ROOSEVELT: Indeed. At the Yalta Conference he kept farting and blaming it on Churchill.

SANTA: Stalin's eyes are like cold, black pools. There's no depth in them. No humanity. No feeling. No sense that they actually perceive anything.

PRESIDENT ROOSEVELT: Eleanor has eyes like that.

SANTA: Hitler has eyes like that.

PRESIDENT ROOSEVELT: Yes. Of course, what you said. Hitler.

SANTA: Speaking of that nutter, he wanted a bunch of religious artifacts and various items dealing with the occult. I'm gonna give him the headpiece to the Staff of Ra. That can't do much harm, right?

PRESIDENT ROOSEVELT: What? Certainly Hitler is on the naughty list? I mean, he's worse than himself!*

SANTA: Of course, of course. And he's a crap painter, obviously . . .

PRESIDENT ROOSEVELT: But?

---

* Historical footnote: This was the first "worse than Hitler" reference ever made.

SANTA: *(long pause)* He's such a good speaker . . .

PRESIDENT ROOSEVELT: Santa!

SANTA: His letter was kind of frightening, as all German letters are, to be honest with you, but then he starts talking and I'm all like, "I shouldn't agree with you, you're so nuts, but boy you get me all fired up!" Don't worry, though, all he's getting is a lump of coal.

PRESIDENT ROOSEVELT: And what about the leader of France?

   (Both men laugh.)

FILED

DEC 2 0 1944

SANTA: Talk about someone who isn't real!

   (Both laugh again.)

PRESIDENT ROOSEVELT: And what of my letter, Santa?

SANTA: Yes, Mr. President, that's why I'm here. It was so earnest.

PRESIDENT ROOSEVELT: Your workshop produces millions of toy trains—I can only imagine what you could do for America's war machine.

SANTA: Mr. President, I'm sorry, but Santa's magic doesn't work on anything but toys. The tools of war, even in a just cause such as yours, would destroy me. My power is meant to bring joy to children across the world—be they Allies or Axis. You have my support, and I will make toys that champion the American cause like Monopoly and Lincoln Logs, but that is all.

PRESIDENT ROOSEVELT: I understand.

SANTA: As for the rest of your letter . . . ho ho ho! Ol' Santa might have just what you asked for! My only question is, how do I fit "ramps" under your Christmas tree?

Santa was left alone after this and through the rest of World War II (FDR got his ramps—instead of a vaccine to cure polio that Santa was going to give him). However, the Cold War brought new demands from our government. The atomic bomb and the subsequent space race fueled a desperate need for major advances in technology. But what was really needed was magic. The top scientists all agreed: There is only one source for legitimate magic (two if you count the Amazing Kreskin)—and that is Santa Claus.

During the 1950s, the U.S. government became obsessed with capturing Santa in order to learn the source of his magic, conduct tests on him, and convince him to serve the United States. Numerous offer letters went out to him, promising him everything under the sun. However, he never even bothered to respond. It didn't help that some of the letters were actually recycled empty promises that had been made to the Indians.

TO: ~~CHIEF FLOWING WATER OF THE PONCA TRIBE~~ SANTA CLAUS
FROM: THE UNITED STATES GOVERNMENT
DATE: ~~1858~~ 1950

Dear ~~Chief Flowing Water~~, SANTA,

In return for your cooperation and access to ~~your territories~~ THE NORTH POLE we will provide you with:

New land.
Cash payment for 30 years.
Mills to grind grain and saw wood.
An interpreter, miller, mill engineer and a farmer.
Blankets that are absolutely not infected with any sort of communicable disease.

We Promise!

Santa wasn't having it. Action would need to be taken.

May 2, 1951

Dear Mr. Claus:

I write following my earlier correspondence regarding my offer of employment; a letter to which no response was received.

After intense negotiations with the Department of War (I really went to bat for you), I am now in a position to provide for you the following:

1.) $12,500 per year (I'm sure that will sound lousy in 2013 or something but trust me, that's a lot of money in these times)

2.) Unlimited Premberton Brand Pipe Tobacco (in exchange for a small ad on your sled)

3.) "Around the World in One Night" access to Grace Kelly

All we ask is that you show up for meetings in Washington, D.C., once per month, provide our engineers with unlimited access to the North Pole for research and study, and give us three sleds with enough power to deliver a payload to carry a W87 MX missile.

Also, How easy is it to cross the border to Russia from the Arctic Circle? Asking for a friend.

Please extend this letter the courtesy of a response. I may have dropped atomic bombs on Hiroshima and Nagasaki but rest assured I'm a peaceful man and would certainly never want to take aggressive action against you. However, there are forces in the government with less wisdom than I.

Regards,

Harry Truman

Harry Sagittarius (I don't know why people think the "S" doesn't stand for anything) Truman

PRIVATE

Letter from Harry S Truman to Santa Claus

In early 1954, the government transformed an abandoned former auxiliary airfield into a facility of unparalleled grandeur and secrecy. What was informally called "North Pole, Nevada" was changed to the simpler "Area 51," a playground for scientists and military engineers to focus on all things Santa. And it had its share of successes. In early January 1971, Blitzen was briefly captured while on reindeer shore leave (time off after Christmas that Santa gives all of his servants to recuperate from the holidays) after visiting a caribou mistress he had stashed away in northern Wyoming.

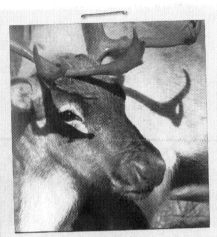

PEGGY –
BLITZEN'S FAVORITE BOU-TY CALL

Walrus Team Four, the heavily mustachioed 1970s version of SEAL Team Six, captured Blitzen on an anonymous tip and held him for twenty-four hours before legally having to release him. Imagine all we could've learned if we had just ignored his right to not be detained without cause . . . like we would do today. (In the 1970s, "enhanced interrogation" meant raising your voice.) We were so primitive back then! So married to the "Constitution" like a big bunch of squares!*

Fortunately, the government was able to run enough tests on the magical flying beast that we gained valuable insight that would lead to technological advances that many of our adversaries still do not have today, most notably stealth flight. All of Santa's reindeer have the magical ability to fly without sound (with the exclusion of reindeer farts, an unfortunate side effect of genetically modified magic corn). Army scientists were able to isolate the genetic source of stealth power within a reindeer and replicate it. Long story short: Every stealth plane in the United States military is fueled by a derivative of reindeer bone marrow.

---

* The Constitution was one of this country's most cherished documents. It was retired in 2019 after an online petition to mothball it received the required 350,000 signatures.

In 1989, former Oakland A's* star Jose Canseco injected himself with reindeer bone marrow that he got from a dancer at an all-nude party held in Madonna's basement. The effects of this are still unknown, but legend has it that some nights you can see what locals call "a bloated Cuban with teeny-tiny testicles" soaring above San Francisco Bay.

But that was the extent of any contact between Santa Claus and the United States heading into 2013. While the government was still anxious to study Santa and show Fidel Castro who was boss, the Cold War had diverted its attention. The assassination of John F. Kennedy in 1963 was the final nail in the coffin (not Kennedy's coffin, the Santa-pursuit coffin). Kennedy's goal of capturing Santa and making him watch Marilyn Monroe shower with him was never going to be realized. Without admitting as much, the government had essentially given up. Most of its clandestine programs were abandoned and the pursuit of Santa was filed in the "Crap We Don't Care About Anymore" cabinet, right in front of "Space Program" and right behind "Fourth Amendment."

Fifty years later, the beast awoke.

It all started with an innocuous email. Or, what should have been an innocuous email. Just a casual email between friends, really, and that should have been the end of it because it was nothing more than that: a note between friends. If sometime in your life you had a pen pal named Sally you would have written Sally a cute little letter and sent it to her in England or wherever she might have lived, and Sally would have received your letter and opened it and cherished it for some period of time until you were no longer pen pals. The letter would have been stored in a shoe box and made it to a closet eventually and then moved to a home and another home. At some point Sally, now middle-aged and not happy with her post-child-bearing weight gain, would come across the letter, think fondly of her youth and of you for a brief moment, and toss it into the trash.

— Did You Know? —
ChRistmas tRees feel pain.

* The Oakland A's used to be a baseball team.

Alas, in 2013, things were different. Private correspondence between two individuals was not really private. If you sent a letter to your pen pal Sally in those days it most likely was not a letter at all—it was an email. That email, which you intended for Sally's eyes only, was also read by upwards of fifteen different government agencies under the auspices of "keeping Sally safe," which was just code for "we don't want to deal with getting a warrant." The only thing America's government was efficiently doing in 2013 was discarding notions of privacy and liberty in return for the illusion of security.

Why would the NSA read your personal emails? No one really knows, because the NSA is kind of like your uncle who served in Vietnam: They'd really rather not talk about it.

Before long, the greatest intelligence apparatus the world had ever seen went from scrutinizing exchanges between Vladimir & Ivan and Mahmoud & Yusef to harvesting the correspondence between Brad & Lauren, Joe & Daria, and most important for our purposes: Matt & Sally.

-----Original Message-----

To: Sally Pearson <sallywags88@gmail.com>
From: Matt Podalski <heyitsmattLOL@hotmail.com>
Sent: November 19, 2013 11:14AM
Subject: YOU BETTER WATCH OUT!!!

Santa Claus is coming from the north pole soon are you noddy or nice? I hope he gets me a BIG BOOMER! Hope you don't get COLE!
xxoox matt

Now, had this email been an old-fashioned letter, this is where the story would have ended. Sally would've gotten her letter and the United States Postal Service would've gotten forty-four cents closer to closing its slight $15 billion annual budget gap, and everyone would've lived happily ever after (except for the Postal Service, which is seriously screwed up). Instead, as soon as Matt hit "send," this innocuous email made its way down the Information Superhighway on its way to Sally's inbox. Before arriving, though, it made a few pit stops along the way, most notably to Brandon C. Douglas of the National Security Agency.

Now, *you* have the advantage of knowing that Matt Podalski is a harmless young boy who can't spell very well and that Sally is his slightly older pen pal. But Brandon C. Douglas does not. Not knowing all the details is a problem you're going to face when sucking up billions of emails and looking for what you think might be red flags. The proverbial needle in a needle-stack, as it were.

The first red flag, as you may have guessed, was the threatening tone. YOU BETTER WATCH OUT is not grammatically correct (YOU'D BETTER WATCH OUT would please your teacher more) but it is worrisome to an agency tasked with flagging threats. And to read that someone or some *thing* was coming from the North Pole, well, that's worrisome as well. And when that thing that's coming might be a BIG BOOMER then your worries multiply even more. Especially if you don't have the luxury of knowing that a BIG BOOMER is a cheap, plastic bazooka that shoots delicious marshmallows, and looks like this:

Unbeknownst to Brandon C. Douglas of the NSA, the word COLE did not in fact refer to the 2000 bombing of the USS *Cole,* carried out by Al Qaeda. Rather, it was due to an eight-year-old being unable to spell COAL correctly. That may or may not be the fault of his teacher,[*] but that's a subject for a different book entirely. Regardless, eight-year-old Matt Podalski's innocent note to his pen pal was cause for alarm. At least to Brandon C. Douglas:

To: Roger Kimmons <roger.kimmons@nsa.gov>
From: Douglas Brandon <douglas.brandon@nsa.gov>
Sent: November 20, 2013 2:27AM
Subject: North Pole

Roger -
What do we know about the terms "Santa Claus" or the "north pole"? -DB

To: Douglas Brandon <douglas.brandon@nsa.gov>
From: Roger Kimmons <roger.kimmons@nsa.gov>
Sent: November 21, 2013 8:33AM
Subject: Re: North Pole

Santa Claus could be referencing Santa Claus I suppose. Or it could be a code name for an operative. North pole could be a geographic reference. Hard to say without knowing the context. Can't hurt to send me the correspondence in question and I'll take a look.

Rog

Of course, saying something *can't* hurt doesn't always mean that particular thing can't hurt. In fact, the inverse is often the case. *It can't hurt* have no doubt been the last words uttered before the demise of countless individuals since the dawn of man. *It can't hurt* to tell the emperor how I really feel. *It can't hurt* to pull up to that pirate ship and ask for directions. *It can't hurt* to light a match and see where that gas odor is coming from. So, figuring it couldn't hurt, Douglas sent the email in question to

---

[*] Actually it is *totally* the teacher's fault, but Mrs. Huntington can't be fired.

his boss, Roger. Poor eight-year-old Matt Podalski had no idea he was now an unwitting accomplice in the creation of the greatest threat Christmas had ever faced: clueless bureaucrats.

It wasn't long before great minds, or just minds, really, pored over every detail of the letter in the hopes of deciphering its meaning. To cover their bases, Santa Claus was now under the watchful gaze of the federal government.

It's probably hard for folks to understand these days, but back in the early twenty-first century—like around 2013 or so—people still had an expectation of privacy. It was considered uncouth (and usually even illegal) to snoop through people's things without any legal justification! Can you imagine? People used to get upset about that sort of thing. Zany!

One of the first tasks facing the NSA was to establish where the North Pole was. Education be not so good in this country, in large part thanks to a government effort to make education good in this country. If reading, writing, and 'rithmetic had fallen by the wayside since Jimmy Carter's creation of the Department of Education, then geography had fallen by the wayside and rolled down an embankment into a gully. Most folks understood the North Pole to be "norther" than their current location but many were unsure what their current location was. So the intrepid investigators did what you do these days when you have a question about anything: They typed "north pole" into Google Maps.

Armed with a satellite view of what they imagined to be Santa's secret staging ground for *God knows what,* the United States government opened up a file and began a "harmless" investigation into Santa Claus. It wasn't the only reason Santa Claus would soon find himself in the government's crosshairs. Another reason was an eight-year-old Jewish boy. His name was Mark Weinstein, and he loved his sister enough to write a heartfelt letter to one of the dumbest people ever to somehow stumble his way into the Capitol.

2.

YES, HANK JOHNSON, THERE IS A
SANTA CLAUS

Dear Congressman Johnson,
I am in the 4th grade. My sister just finished
kindergarten and did real good. I said that
Santa Claus should come early this year as a
reward, but my mom said he only comes one
day a year. But I think if he knew how hard
Sarah worked he would want to give her a
toy. Mommy had a bottle of her red grape
sleeping juice and said, "Why don't you write
a letter to our Congressman and ask him?"
before taking a nap on the kitchen floor.
So. . . since you're a powerful person, do
you know Santa Claus? Or do you know how
I can reach him?
Thank you!
Mark Weinstein
4th grade

H ank Johnson's chief of staff read the letter and grinned the biggest grin he'd grinned in a long time. It wasn't easy being chief of staff for one of the dumbest congressmen ever to not grace the halls of Congress. It was a lot of damage control. A lot of shrugging of shoulders. A lot of shaking of heads. And a lot of wanting to find something to distract people from your stupid, stupid boss. At this moment, Ron Martirano held that very thing in his hands.

From the office of

Hank Johnson
U.S. Representative for Georgia's
Fourth Congressional District

2240 Rayburn HOB
Washington, DC 20515
Phone: (202) 225-1605
Fax: (202) 226-0691

Lithonia Office
5700 Hillandale Dr.,
Suite 120
Lithonia, GA 30058
Phone: (770) 987-2291
Fax: (770) 987-87211

Congress of the United States
House of Representatives
Washington, DC 20515

INTERNAL USE ONLY

To: Hank Johnson (D - GA)
From: Ron Martirano, Rep. Johnson's Chief of Staff
Date: June 20, 2013
Re: Opportunity

Sir, we just got a truly sweet and touching letter from a 4th grader who has requested a visit from Santa Claus for his sister. I read it and I cried, because it's the perfect piece of nonsense that we can use to our advantage.

I have a number of ideas on how to best use this, including as a way to distract from that horrific newspaper article that came out last week about you. And with a last name like Weinstein, I think it's safe to say that Santa won't be answering this kid's letter. Though it's weird someone named Weinstein lives in your incredibly gerrymandered district.

Let's meet at your earliest possible convenience to discuss this matter.

Sincerely,

Ron Martirano

Ron Martirano

Ron fired off the memo and waited for the congressman's response. Then he got a sinking feeling in his stomach. He knocked on the congressman's door.

"Come enter in," said Hank Johnson.

"Sir, you can say 'come in' or 'enter' but it's not necessary to say 'come enter in,'" said Ron.

"Yes okay affirmative," said Hank.

Ron sighed. "I emailed you a memo. I was wondering if you got it," Ron asked.

"Computer's still sleeping I'm afraid," said Hank.

"Sir, you just have to wake it. Never mind. Here, read this."

Ron placed the front page of the *Atlanta Journal-Constitution* in front of the congressman and returned to his desk. The following took Hank Johnson twenty-seven minutes to read, not including two lengthy bathroom breaks:

Saturday, June 15, 2013

The Atlanta Journal-Constitution

Credible. Compelling. Complete.

BREAKING NEWS
A.1 DAY AT AJC.COM

WEATHER $1

now
71 / 88
Cloudy early,
more sun later

79 / 85
Partly cloudy
and warm

Congressman Johnson's Mental Fitness Questioned by Own Doctor

CONGRESSMAN "DANGEROUSLY STUPID"

by Matt Fisher and Jon Bershad

Doctor Erik Rehder is scared. The 58-year-old medical practitioner has delivered babies, conducted surgeries, and performed under the most stressful of circumstances without flinching. But when he thinks about his former patient, Congressman Hank Johnson (D-GA), he breaks into a cold sweat.

"I had read all of the stories about Mr. Johnson—how he feared that the island of Guam would 'capsize' and such, and his speech about helium. I just figured that he was kind of dim," the flustered doctor admitted. "But then I was working the ER at Grady when he came in complaining of chest pains. I asked him when the pains started and he said right when he began sticking pins in his chest." Doctor Rehder paused, shaking his head. "This is a man who makes rules and things. And I'm truly worried he gets paid more than I do . . ." the doctor said, his voice trailing off.

After removing the pins Dr. Rehder stayed with Congressman Johnson for a few hours to monitor him. What he witnessed firsthand shocked him.

"About half an hour later Congressman Johnson started to turn blue. I thought to myself, 'Oh my God, is he choking on the extra toy he asked for in his Happy Meal?' But it turns out that he forgot to breathe in. Apparently he has to write notes to himself to remember to breathe in and out, which he claims he needs because he's not good at 'planning ahead.'" At this point in the interview Dr. Rehder slammed his fists on a table and pointed directly at me.

"You have to report this! This man gets to vote in the United States Congress! He has a say on our budget, on our health care, on declaring war.*

"I recommended to Congressman Johnson's family that his IQ is likely in the high forties, and that he not be allowed to do things like operate a motor vehicle, or for that matter operate silverware. I think it's time that the voters know this about their representative before it's too late."

FOR MORE ON CONGRESSMAN JOHNSON'S ALLEGED HORRIFIC INCOMPETENCE, PLEASE TURN TO PAGES A4–A11

---

* In olden days, United States presidents would go through the constitutionally mandated process of asking Congress to declare war before fighting in one.

Not a short while later, Ron received what his boss referred to as an "email memo but on paper."

To: Ron
From: Me
Date: Tuesday?
Re: tard. Ha ha ha ha! Look what I did there!

M E M O

Ron, your memmo thingy had like a billion words in it and I could only get thru the first sentance or two. Your a smart guy -- just do whatever is best.

Weinstein? Is that Irish?

Judge Judy starts in a few minutes and then it's nap time, so I gotta go. Talk soon.

Oh, and I read the other parts of the newspaper that was so mean to me and found something that we might be able to use.

GARFUNKEL

I'M GONNA EAT THIS LASAGNA!

...YUP!

THIS MADE ME LAUGH! BUT IS THIS NEWS? I THINK THIS MIGHT BE SOMETHING!!!

Ron took a deep breath and reminded himself that someday he would be dead. In the meantime, he felt it his duty to look out for the best interests of his boss. He got on the phone, which Hank called "the nonmusic boom box."

Transcript of telephone call between Ron Martirano,
Congressman Johnson's chief of staff, and Debbie Wasserman
Schultz, chair of the Democratic National Committee.

Taken from audiotapes made by Mr. Martirano of all
official business conducted on behalf of Hank Johnson
for whatever "giant legal mess he's inevitably going to
get into in the future."

7:54pm — 8:25pm

Secretary: Congresswoman Schultz's office. May I help you?

Ron: Ron Martirano for Debbie.

Secretary: One moment please. (slight pause) I'm fine being
a male secretary for a woman.

Ron: Okay. Great. As well you should be.

Secretary: (slight pause) I'm totally fine with it.
My online dating profile says "Occupation:
Secretary" and I've had lots of dates with
confused lesbians.

Ron: This is getting weird. May I speak with Debbie now?

Secretary: Sure. Like I said, I'm fine with switching
traditional gender roles.

Ron: You're not fine with it, right?

Secretary: Right. I'll get Debbie.

Debbie: Ron! Oh sweet mercy, what has he done now? Has
he accidentally killed someone?

Ron: Not anyone new, no.

Debbie: Oh, thank God. I still remember the time he
almost drowned in that rainstorm.

Ron: I told him not to keep his mouth open as he was
looking up.

Debbie: Well, what can I help you with?

Ron: We got a letter from some Jewish kid asking for
help getting in touch with Santa Claus and it
dawned on me. Are you ready?

Debbie: Sure.   —cont.—

Ron:	Santa is never going to grant this kid's wish because of religious intolerance.
Debbie:	(Pause) Ron, that's insane. Santa Claus deals with Christian boys and girls because Christmas is a Christian holiday. That's not intolerant, it's just the rules of individual religions. If we started going after Santa for every little religious slight, or every silly little law he breaks, it would be such an incredible distraction for the American people . . . (slight gasp) Ron, that's absolutely genius.
Ron:	Thank you. Just think of how we can use this— if Santa is "screwing everyone over," then who wants to read about a bad economy?
Debbie:	Or embassy attacks in Damascus, Cairo, and Ottawa that we've kept hidden . . .
Ron:	Ottawa?
Debbie:	Nothing. Ron, thank you for coming to me with this. The president and I will not forget this, especially as we begin to put together a short list for cabinet jobs for a third term.
Ron:	Third term? Excuse me?
Debbie:	Nothing. Please send me this kid's letter immediately. Bye.

Debbie, unaccustomed to hearing good ideas, immediately called a special meeting of Very Important People. And Joe Biden.

— Did You Know? —
Santa Refuses to deliver gifts to anyone named Manilow in case they're Related to Barry.

DEMOCRATIC NATIONAL COMMITTEE

MEETING MINUTES OF JUNE 24, 2013

PRESENT

BARACK OBAMA, President of the United States

JOE BIDEN, Vice President of the United States

DEBBIE WASSERMAN SCHULTZ, Chairwoman of the DNC

DENIS McDONOUGH, President Obama's Chief of Staff

JACK LEW, Treasury Secretary

GEORGE CLOONEY, Handsome Actor

ERIC HOLDER, Attorney General of the United States

CALL TO ORDER

Chairwoman Debbie Wasserman Schultz opened the meeting at 8:30 A.M.

SECRETARY'S MINUTES

Minutes of May were approved. Secretary asked to be called "Administrative Assistant" because "secretary" is offensive for some reason.

TREASURER'S REPORT

Jack Lew kept trying to impress everyone with his "kooky" signature. Very annoying.

CHAIRWOMAN'S REPORT

Debbie Wasserman Schultz opened a discussion on the usefulness of a multi-year media distraction to ensure that the American public doesn't focus on any current or future failings and/or scandals of the administration. Vice President Biden became immediately defensive, saying, "That's my job!" and then asked the president to "pull my finger." The president, for the fourth time that week, then called for the Sergeant-at-Arms to have Biden forcibly removed from the room.

-1-

DEMOCRATIC NATIONAL COMMITTEE

MEETING MINUTES OF JUNE 24, 2013

Wasserman Schultz then proceeded to lay out what she called the Case Against Santa Claus.

President Obama took to the Santa Claus concept immediately, as he had "plans for a number of terribly illegal scandals" over the coming years. He appointed Chief of Staff Denis McDonough to begin brainstorming ideas for how to take advantage of any and all ways to exploit the matter in the administration's favor.

Vice President Biden, who had apparently bored the Sergeant-at-Arms literally to death* with a story about Amtrak, rejoined the meeting just in time to say something vaguely racist about Asians** before the "Santa Claus" measure was to be officially decided upon.

MOTION TO ACCEPT: President Obama.

SECONDED: VP Biden.

POINTED OUT THAT IT'S UNNECESSARY TO HAVE ANYTHING "SECONDED" ONCE THE PRESIDENT MAKES A DECISION: Eric Holder.

COMFORTED JOE BIDEN: George Clooney.

OTHER POINTS OF BUSINESS

• President Obama approved the hiring of a new body double who will pretend to go to church for him "on whatever day we Christians go to church."

---

* Officially the cause of death was listed as "tedium-inspired cerebral hemorrhage."
** When told that the Japanese drive on the other side of the road, Biden asked, "On purpose or because they're terrible drivers?"

-2-

DEMOCRATIC NATIONAL COMMITTEE

MEETING MINUTES OF JUNE 24, 2013

- Vice President Biden used twenty-seven curse words during the meeting—a new record. Swear Jar now up to over $83,000. Almost enough to buy a Tesla.

- A year to the day after the president's official taxidermist finished his work, debate continued on whether to reveal that Osama bin Laden was stuffed and on display in the Green Room of the White House. Decision was postponed.

- At one point, Vice President Biden turned to Debbie Wasserman Schultz and said, "Hey, sweetie, can you please get me a seltzer and an egg salad sandwich?" When it was pointed out that Wasserman Schultz was not a secretary or homely waitress, Biden apologized profusely and said her hair "looked like lightning."

- The president plugged his ears and said "La La La La" really loudly so he wouldn't overhear the discussion on which conservatives the IRS would be intimidating in July. It was decided to "just start going through voter rolls alphabetically. But let's make sure we get John *Boner* twice." Everyone laughed, including the president, at the hilarious mispronunciation of Speaker Boehner's name. Clooney is *so* handsome when he laughs.

- Vice President Biden pinched George Clooney's butt and was forcibly removed by the (new) Sergeant-at-Arms. Claims the move is called a "Delaware handshake."

- Treasury Secretary Lew reintroduced his plan to stimulate the economy by Quantitative Easing. Biden asked for no big words and was told Quantitative Easing means "printing buttloads of money." President Obama praised Lew. Biden laughed at "buttloads." Lew made a scribble and said it was his address.

- President Obama signed another five hundred thousand blank pardons for White House staffers "just in case."

-3-

Debbie immediately got on the nonmusical boom box and called Congressman Johnson's chief of staff.

It wasn't more than a day before Congressman Johnson's fist had been removed from his mouth and he was back at "work."

Ron knocked on Hank's office door.

"Come in entering," said Hank.

"Congressman, great news!"

Hank shushed him and pointed to the sleeping computer. Normally Ron would have taken the time to explain how electronics work to the congressman but he had too much to do. "Congressman," Ron said in a hushed tone so as not to wake his boss's computer, "I need you to fight on behalf of a young little boy for whom there is no Christmas. Are you willing to help me do that?"

"I am?"

"I'm asking if you're willing to fight on behalf of a young boy who would be denied Christmas solely based on his religion."

"You are?"

"Sir, this doesn't have to be so hard. It really doesn't. I just need you to say yes."

"Yes okay affirmative."

People didn't appreciate it at the time, but at least now we have perspective from so many years after Hank Johnson's death. The Hank Johnson Museum of Unintentional Hilarity in Atlanta is well worth a visit. It turns out he may have been one of the funniest politicians ever—and he had no idea! He choked to death on oxygen in 2019.

FROM THE DESK OF
CONGRESSMAN HANK JOHNSON
★★★

Deer Mark,

Thank you for your letter. Unfortunately, I don't know Santa Claus personally. However, I do know that Santa is much like Iranian President Mackmood Admiral Ackbar in that he is not a fan of Jews like you. Santa doesn't give presents to Jews or Jewesses like your sister, probably on account of you all having so much money anyway.

Irregardless, this makes me so mad, and I am going to make sure that this religious bigotry is brought to an end. You're a real champion, my little Jew friend. Thank you for being the ~~impatus~~ ~~impitis~~ force that brings this to into the national spotlight.

Yours,
Hank Johnson
Congressman! Really!

Ron was so excited he personally took the letter to the Capitol Hill Post Office. It was closed because of sequestration, so he wandered around half of Washington looking for a mailbox. Eventually he found one, and after a quiet mugging was able to send it on its way.

Now it was time to sit back and wait. It didn't take long. Several days later a letter with a familiar child's handwriting came addressed to Hank Johnson. Ron placed it on Hank's desk. Hank looked at it.

"Hank Johnson? I remember reading something about that guy. . . ."

"Sir, that's your name. You just need to open the envelope."

"I see that he added some lines under the name. Like a street and a city and things."

"Yes sir, that's an address. That's how letters get places."

"Well I'll be," said Hank.

Hank opened up a desk drawer. Inside were 115 letters addressed only to "GRAMMAW." They had all been returned to sender.

Ron sighed. "Do you know your grandma's address?" he asked.

Hank looked up to heaven. Ron opened Mark Weinstein's letter for him.

Dear Congressman Johnson,

I've made a huge mistake in contacting you. Please leave me out of this.

Santa Claus is awesome and my parents let us celebrate Christmas, too.

They're totally laid back Jews, like 90% of Jews. Don't ruin Christmas.

Yours in deep fear,
Mark Weinstein

P.S. I think you use the term "Jew" more than I think you need to.

Little Mark Weinsten hadn't expected to be contacted by his congressman, again, but little Mark Weinstein didn't really know Hank.

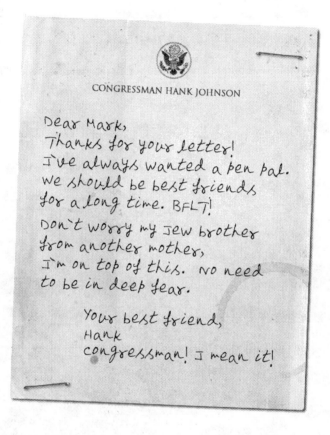

CONGRESSMAN HANK JOHNSON

Dear Mark,
Thanks for your letter!
I've always wanted a pen pal.
We should be best friends
for a long time. BFLT!
Don't worry my Jew brother
from another mother,
I'm on top of this. No need
to be in deep fear.

    Your best friend,
    Hank
    congressman! I mean it!

For all Ron cared, Hank could spend the rest of his term sending letters to Mark. The little boy had served his purpose.

- Did You Know? -
Santa was bullied as a child,
before it was trendy.

USA TODAY™ 07.08.13

BASEBALL
WHO'S NOT ON THE JUICE
8C

A GANNETT COMPANY

This is the Canadian flag, NOT the American flag

NEWS Troubling Rumors Out of Ottawa

Tensions mysteriously rise with our neighbors to the north. **14A**

NEWS Words Most Associated with HOT DOGS

Study by the National Hot Dogs Vendors Association of America. **12B**

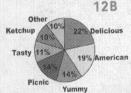

Other 10%
Ketchup 10%
Tasty 11%
14%
Picnic
Yummy 14%
22% Delicious
19% American

Georgia Pol Claims Discrimination

by Mark Steven David Harris

ATLANTA, GA—Hank Johnson (D-GA) stood on the House floor today and accused beloved holiday icon Santa Claus of religious discrimination in ignoring a local Jewish boy who somehow lived in his incredibly gerrymandered district.

"This poor Jew child, who wanted nothing more than a present for his sister, or Jew sister as he might call her, must wake up every day in an America that tolerates this sort of discriminatory behavior in its magical gift-giving. No longer should we allow Christmas to be just about Christ. What about Ganeshmas, or Allahmas, or L. Ron Hubbardmas? We need to be more including with our holidays. They should not be occasions to discriminate. You should not be able to discriminate on someone because of their race or religion or mental power."

A confused and somewhat angry crowd murmured as an oblivious Congressman Johnson rambled on, his aides nervously shuffling their feet on the side of the stage. But the performance was captivating. Later, President Obama sent a mixed message, as he both distanced himself from the remarks and partially embraced them. It was a skill he'd ac-

quired as a veteran of condemning things he supported. Like Guantanamo and drones and transparency and whistle-blowing and marijuana reform.

"While I'd prefer he tone down the rhetoric, Congressman Johnson is indeed correct. Correct that we need to be more tolerant of other religions, especially Islam, which I again want to point out is a beautiful religion whose message has been taken over by a few, six or seven, people on the fringe. I would like to apologize for whatever it is that makes you mad about America."

As for Christmas, Obama stated, "I'm sure this is something that Santa Claus can look into and fix so it is no longer a problem. Clearly if the institution of marriage and the Boy Scouts can make reforms, he can, too. The American people and I love Santa and thank him for all of his gifts over the years."

This politically savvy tone differed than the one used by Congressman Johnson, who spoke for more than two hours, stopping only once after somehow swallowing his necktie after "believing it was a Fruit Roll-Up."

"Never let it be said that I don't protect the Jews in my district," Johnson remarked. "All one of them," he continued. And then, puzzlingly, he said, "Hold for laughter." There were varying reports as to what this last comment meant, with some believing that Johnson accidentally read the stage direction off the Teleprompter, while others argued that that was impossible as Johnson can't read.

(Story Continues on Page A2)

Child's Letter Leads to Real Santa Angst

It may not have gone as smoothly as Ron hoped, but now the seed had been planted in the American consciousness. The horses were out of the gate. The train had left the station. The Christie had bitten into the sandwich.

Now it was time to expand, explain, and, most important, exploit this seed for all it was worth.

- Did You Know? -
Santa Regrets the North Pole's Apartheid policies (which were abandoned in 1997)

3.

SOMETHING'S ROTTEN IN THE
STATE OF NANNY

- Did You Know? -
A "Claus" cocktail is two
parts bourbon, one part milk,
one part orange juice and
tastes absolutely horrible.

The plan was afoot, and not a moment too soon. The administration was being plagued by scandals, and not just nonscandals created by hyperpartisan Republicans. This time there were actual bona fide scandals that threatened the reputation of many administration officials. Most importantly, they threatened the reputation of the "most important member of the administration, Barack Obama," thought Barack Obama.

The president picked up the telephone one Tuesday morning and called Chief of Staff Denis McDonough. We know this because of the "Transcribe All Phone Calls" clause of the "America Is Great, Freedom Liberty Patriot Freedom Act," which every member of Congress passed after reading just the title and nothing else. In addition to building a $70 million bridge in Oklahoma, this clause authorized the Department of Homeland Security to intercept all phone calls generated in the United States and deposited $80,000 in Congressman Charlie Rangel's offshore account.

* * * **PHONE TRANSCRIPT** * * *

Tuesday 12 November 2013, 09:22

Obama: Hello, Denis?

Denis: Hello, Mr. President.

Obama: I thought we talked about this, Denis?

Denis: Right! My apologies! What I meant to say was "Hail Obama."

Obama: I'm never going to give you the second n in "Dennis" back if you keep this up.

Denis: I'm sorry, Dear Leader. It won't happen again.

—cont.—

Obama: And what happens if it does?

Denis: You call the Social Security Administration and have them change the first letter in my name to a *P.*

Obama: And what would that mean your new name is? Say it.

Denis: Penis McDonough.

Obama: Nooo. Say it as if your real name was pronounced "Deenis."

Dennis: (Long pause) Peenis McDonough.

Obama: (Giggles.) That's right. Now, let's get down to business. My concern about this whole Santa thing is how popular the guy is. We need to figure out a way to turn the American public against Santa Claus, because right now I doubt even the press would ignore this one for me . . . unless we changed his name to Benghazi Claus.

(Strangely long amount of laughter)

Denis: Hmm . . . that *is* a problem. What we need is to find someone willing to force Americans over to our side.

Obama: Right. Someone who will take an issue and obsess over it with almost OCD-like devotion. But an issue that no normal person would bother with, you know?

Denis: Definitely someone with almost a Napoleon complex type of chip on his shoulder.

Obama: A tiny, annoying person.

Denis: Yes.

Obama: And it would help if he was crazy-ass rich.

Denis: I've got it!

(At the same time)

Obama: Bloomberg!

Denis: Prince!

(Awkward silence)

Denis: Please don't call the Social Security Administration.

Obama: Too late. Go email Bloomberg. We might need to trick him onto our side.

Denis wanted to immediately reach out to Michael Bloomberg but got sidetracked into seeing if the domain penismcdonough.com was taken. It wasn't. He then focused on the task at hand: Recruiting the most annoying mayor in the world for their nefarious purpose.

From: Denis McDonough <DMcDonough@whitehouse.gov>
To: Michael Bloomberg <MayorPoppins@nyc.gov>
Sent: Wed, Nov 13 2013 3:11 pm
Subject: Obesity In America

Dear Mayor Bloomberg,

Denis McDonough, here - President Obama's Chief of Staff. You have long been a brave leader in the war on obesity in America, and the President and First Lady applaud you for that. But we feel that there is much more we can do in order to save Americans from themselves, and that is to remove positive reinforcements of obesity in society (like, say, Santa Claus for example). Would love to pick your brain more. Let's chat.

Sincerely,
Denis

Denis sent his email and awaited a response. While he was awaiting it, he checked to see if @PenisMcDonough was available on Twitter. It was.

To: Denis McDonough <DMcDonough@whitehouse.gov>
From: Michael Bloomberg <MayorPoppins@nyc.gov>
Sent: Thu, Nov 14, 2013 10:05 a.m.
Subject: Obesity In America

Dear Dennis,

I'm sorry I didn't get back to you right away—I'm working on a new law that would make it illegal for New Yorkers to chew ice. We need to protect our children's enamel.

I'm excited and honored that you've asked me to help with you fight the war against obesity. Count me in! Here are some ideas I've started brainstorming:

1) What if we edited Chris Farley out of Tommy Boy entirely? If we destroy the idea of the "funny fat guy" then we can really turn people against TA's (shorthand for Tubby Americans). Farley, Belushi, Candy—all dead. Coincidence?

2) I could just buy and burn all of the chocolate in the world. Problem solved?

3) In the vein of gun buybacks we could start a cash-for-Nutella program. Though only law-abiding fatties would turn in their Nutella.

4) What if I started the Mayors Against Obesity. MAO—I like that . . .

5) My anti-smoking commercials show deformed people who have been ravaged by various smoking-induced cancers. What if we showed what it's like to be trapped in a fat person's folds?

6) What if we change the slogan "Snickers Really Satisfies" to something like "Snickers Really Contains Pieces of Broken Glass" or "Snickers Gives You AIDS"? I'll run this by my lawyers as it is incredibly libelous.

Oh! What if we got Reverend Al Sharpton to say that a Snickers bar kidnapped a young woman and left her for dead? No! Wait! He can convince inner-city youth to change the popular saying "No Snitches" to "No Snickers." Let me think on that.

Excited to work with you. We'll force America to do what we know is best for them! Legacy!!!

Don't chew ice,

MIKE

Denis was excited at Mayor Bloomberg's enthusiasm. He knew the mayor was an "ideas guy" but had never seen him working firsthand. Before writing a response he checked to see if there was a PenisMcDonough Tumblr page. There wasn't.

-----Original Message-----
To: Michael Bloomberg <MayorPoppins@nyc.gov>
From: Denis McDonough <DMcDonough@whitehouse.gov>

-----Original Message-----
From: Denis McDonough <DMcDonough@whitehouse.gov>
To: Michael Bloomberg <MayorPoppins@nyc.gov>
Cc: Barack Obama <POTUSwiththeMOSTUS@whitehouse.gov>
Sent: Thu, Nov 14, 2013 1:34 pm
Subject: Obesity In America

Dear Mayor Bloomberg,

I'm looping the President in on this email chain.

Love your ideas - especially the one about forming a coalition of mayors. I'll tell Rahm. Question, though - your term ends in approximately seven weeks. Seems unlikely that you can do this if you're no longer a mayor yourself.

Thinking about positive fat role models and, for me, Santa Claus is at the top of the list. Perhaps de-glamorizing Santa would be the best use of your time and assets?

Cheers,
Denis

P.S. - There's only one 'n' in Denis.

The president was "working" in his golf cart when the email from Denis came in. He took a few moments to shoot the mayor an email on his BlackBerry before heading back to the eleventh hole for more work.

---------Original Mesage---------

From: Barack Obama <POTUSwiththeMOSTUS@whitehouse.gov>
To: Michael Bloomberg <MayorPoppins@nyc.gov>
Cc: Denis McDonough <DMcDonough@whitehouse.gov>
Sent: Thu, Nov 14, 2013 2:55 p.m.
Subject: Obesity in America

Great to have you on board, Mayor Bloomberg! Taking time away from an important meeting to respond to you.

While Mao is one of my personal heroes, I think we should perhaps slightly alter the name of your soon-to-be coalition. Maybe Mayors Against Porkers would be better? Mayors United Against Fatty Fats? I don't know, I'm not an ideas guy except when it comes to marketing.

I agree with Denis—Santa Claus is at the top of the list of those responsible for the fattening of America. I'm willing to sanction a study to prove that point to you, and I don't care how much it costs the American taxpayers! That's how serious I am about this. We'll call it "health stimulus" or something.

Let's really get this guy, Mayor Bloomberg. Think of all of the Coca-Cola commercials where Santa guzzles soda in amounts far exceeding 16 oz. Seems almost criminally negligent to me. . . .

It's up to you to save America, Mike. And it will really help to have you spearhead this in the eyes of the public, especially as an independent "Republican"! **ROTFLMAO!!!!!**

Also, let's please steer clear of getting Governor Christie caught up in all of this anti-fatty stuff. Since Hurricane Sandy, that wobbly, short-tempered tub of goo is my homie!

Thanks,
Barack Obama
Two Term President of the United States

P.S.—No biggie, but one n in Denis. Like Penis with a D.

When the email arrived the mayor's phone emitted a tone of not more than 12 decibels. He had mandated a 12-decibel limit to prevent people from being deafened by overly loud message alert tones.* The legislation wasn't popular, but that didn't matter. The mayor knew he was doing the right thing.

He read the email in short, eight-second bursts. He had mandated such short bursts for reading emails to prevent people from straining their eyes by reading for more than eight seconds at a time. The legislation wasn't popular, but that didn't matter. The mayor knew he was doing the right thing.

---

* By the end of 2013, there were 242 deaths attributed to "failure to answer the phone in time."

He thought of big fat Santa quaffing sugary drinks and being a big fat fatty role model to millions of people. And he thought of those millions of children desperately in need of a champion—someone to rise to the occasion and be the boss of them and tell them what to do for their own good. And then he looked at the statue on his desk of a Bloomberg-shaped individual standing on a pile of doughnuts and realized that Obama was right: *He* was the man for the job.

He wrote a response email in short, nine-second bursts. He had mandated such short bursts for writing emails to prevent people from bruising their fingertips for more than nine seconds at a time. The legislation wasn't popular, but that didn't matter. The mayor knew he was doing the right thing.

*** EMAIL ***

-----Original Message-----
From: Michael Bloomberg <MayorPoppins@nyc.gov>
To: Denis McDonough <DMcDonough@whitehouse.gov>
Cc: Barack Obama <POTUSwiththeMOSTUS@whitehouse.gov>
Sent: Thu, Nov 14, 2013 4:18 pm
Subject: Obesity In America

Dear Mr. President and Dennis,

Ooooh! Just thinking of Santa drinking all of that soda, thumbing his nose at me, makes my blood boil, and for someone of my size (3'9" in stilt-shoes) that is incredibly dangerous.

I am ALL IN — let's take Santa down!

Mayors Against Porkers seems confusing. I like how "Mayors Against Fatties" rolls off the tongue...like bacon bits roll off the tongue of Adele. LOL!

She has a big bum and must always be eating bacon bits!

As for Dennis's concern that I won't be mayor of New York for much longer. . . I've been thinking about that and have some ideas. I'll figure it out.

Now if you'll excuse me, I have to run off for a meeting with the city council. I'm trying to enact an 8 pm curfew throughout New York. The City That Never Sleeps needs to get eight full hours of sleep per night. That's just good common sense.

Enthusiastically Yours,
M.B.

P.S. - I refuse to spell "Dennis" with one 'n' - it creeps me out.

P.P.S.—If it's after 8 p.m. PLEASE GO TO BED.

The mayor thought long and hard about what Denis had said. He liked being mayor. He liked being called "mayor." If he was no longer mayor, people would go back to calling him "lil' fella." He couldn't let that happen.

Then he had an idea. On his wall was a map of the United States. He picked up a dart and threw it at the map. The dart fell to the floor because he'd outlawed pointy darts, but it had made a small mark near a city on the map. He believed this was his fate.

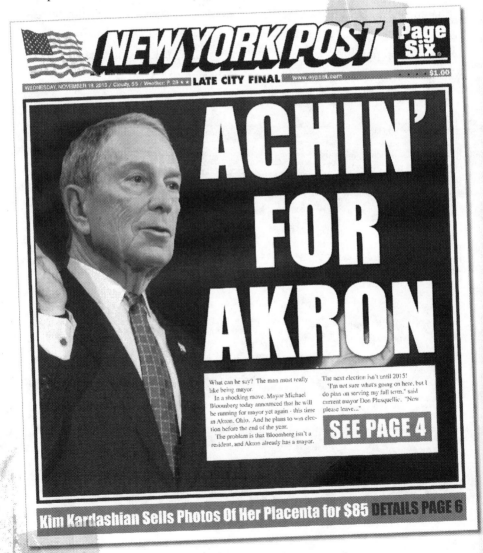

They say money can't buy you happiness, and Mike knew that to be true. Look at Donald Trump, he thought. The most miserable bastard in the whole world. But Mike knew money could buy mayorships. And mayorships could buy happiness. And he was determined to try.

MAYOR MIKE FAILS IN BID AT BUYING AKRON CONSTITUTION

The first sign of trouble was when an ad on Akron Craigslist appeared offering "big $$$ for historical documents." Soon, messages from the same user, MayorMikeyB, started popping up all over the website that made it clear: Someone was trying to buy the Akron Constitution.

"Weirdest damn thing I've ever seen," said Matt Yaeger, the site administrator for the website. "The guy kept posting ads offering a king's ransom...

[CONTINUE]

Comments (12,517) | Shares (2,139) | Michael Bloomberg

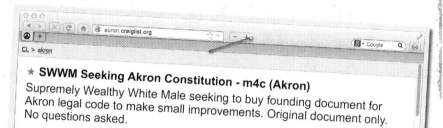

★ SWWM Seeking Akron Constitution - m4c (Akron)

Supremely Wealthy White Male seeking to buy founding document for Akron legal code to make small improvements. Original document only. No questions asked.

- Location: NYC
- It's NOT O.K. to contact this poster with services or other commercial interests
- It IS O.K. to contact this poster if you are Nicolas Cage

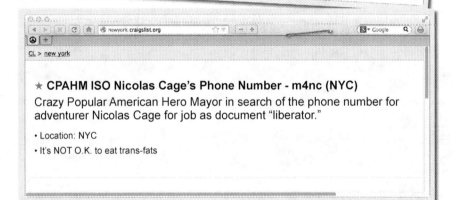

★ CPAHM ISO Nicolas Cage's Phone Number - m4nc (NYC)

Crazy Popular American Hero Mayor in search of the phone number for adventurer Nicolas Cage for job as document "liberator."

- Location: NYC
- It's NOT O.K. to eat trans-fats

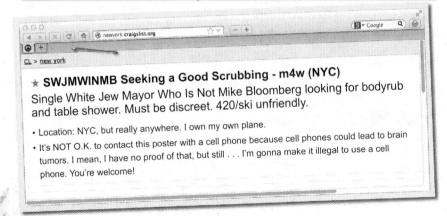

★ SWJMWINMB Seeking a Good Scrubbing - m4w (NYC)

Single White Jew Mayor Who Is Not Mike Bloomberg looking for bodyrub and table shower. Must be discreet. 420/ski unfriendly.

- Location: NYC, but really anywhere. I own my own plane.
- It's NOT O.K. to contact this poster with a cell phone because cell phones could lead to brain tumors. I mean, I have no proof of that, but still . . . I'm gonna make it illegal to use a cell phone. You're welcome!

Mike knew of other sayings, too, not just the one about money not buying happiness. He knew that if at first you don't succeed, try, try again. He didn't know why that saying had "try" twice. He thought one "try" was plenty. In fact, the second "try" was wasteful. In his mind he created a law changing the saying to "If at first you don't succeed, try again." The law made him happy. The citizens in the world inside his head were annoyed. They'd get used to it, he thought.

THE BLAZE

STORIES THEBLAZE TV RADIO MAGAZINE BLOG CONTRIBUTORS BOOKS MARKETPLACE

HOT TOPICS: Egypt | Circus Clown | Domestic Surveillance | Obamacare | #2A | TheBlaze TV

f 421K   ▼ 206K   g+ 29.1K   in 2.9K

DO YOU HAVE YOUR HAZMAT SUIT?   1-800-HAZMATS

LIVE NOW ON THE BLAZE RADIO NETWORK: THE ARMAGEDDON SHOW

MAYOR MIKE MAKES OFFER TO BUY DON PLUSQUELLIC

Nov. 24, 2013 9:02pm | 539 17.6K 5 4 217

In a shocking development out of New York City, Mayor Michael Bloomberg has offered to buy Akron mayor Don Plusquellic for $250 million.

Bloomberg, who last month outlawed smoking at sea within 20 nautical miles of New York for fear of second hand smoke harming dolphins, made the offer in an official letter sent to Plusquellic's office in Akron, Ohio, where Bloomberg is said to have been looking for "large swaths of real estate," according to one unnamed broker.

When reminded that slavery was outlawed by the 13th amendment, the crazy-eyed mayor blurted out, "Ok, what will it cost to have the 13th amendment destroyed? Can someone please get me Nic Cage's f***ing phone number?!"

The offer was tentatively rejected by Mr. Plusquellic.

Click HERE to leave a comment. Click HERE if you're going to rant about Rand or Ron Paul or hysterically quote bible verses and not comment on the preceding story.

THE STORIES

THEBLAZETV – 804 DAYS OF CONSECUTIVE PROGRAMMING WITHOUT A SINGLE PERSON WHO FUNDAMENTALLY DISAGREES WITH ONE ANOTHER

"THIS PRESIDENT WANTS TO MURDER YOUR FAMILY" – A THANKSGIVING MESSAGE FROM GLENN BECK.

Absent the constitution of Akron, and with a sitting mayor who seemed uninterested in not being mayor anymore, Mike made the only move that made any sense from the perspective of a tiny, hectoring billionaire.

"All the News That's Fit to Print"

The New York Times

VOL. CLVII .. No. 54,167 +   © 2013 The New York Times   NEW YORK, WEDNESDAY, NOVEMBER 27, 2013 $5 beyond the greater New York metropolitan area $4.0

Bloomberg Purchases Akron
Professional Mayor's Bold, Unprecedented Move

AKRON - After nine days of seemingly absurd rumors about outgoing New York City Mayor Michael Bloomberg, the New York Times has learned that Mr. Bloomberg has bought the 62+ square miles of land that encompass the city of Akron, Ohio, and installed himself as mayor.

"I have big plans for Akron, and more importantly, for the nation," an ebullient Bloomberg said in a statement. (Note: If you're one of the hayseeds in the flyover states, "ebullient" means "stoked." But what are the odds one of you yokels is reading the New York Times? Ha! We laugh at you!)

"First and foremost, I plan to keep running Mayors Against Illegal Guns to help rid this country of the scourge of illegal, constitutionally protected guns. But I have even bigger plans than

that, which I look forward to sharing with you when the time comes."

Upon officially closing the potentially questionable deal to buy an American city from the federal government, Mr. Bloomberg summarily fired current mayor Don Plusquellic, the human being whom he had tried to purchase just days earlier. Mr. Plusquellic was unavailable for comment, as all traces of him and his family have been wiped from existence.

Mr. Bloomberg made the announcement on Bloomberg (no relation) Television. (Just kidding about the no relation thing. Eighteen years as a New York Times writer and I've never had fun. Not once. Until today. Consider this my two weeks notice.)

Upon hearing the news, the president rested his nine-iron against Joe Biden's leg and dictated an email.

– Did You Know? –
Santa's close friends call him K.K.

---------Original Mesage---------

From: Barack Obama <POTUSwiththeMOSTUS@whitehouse.gov>
To: Michael Bloomberg <MayorPoppins@nyc.gov>
Cc: Denis McDonough <DMcDonough@whitehouse.gov>
Sent: Thu, Nov 28, 2013 3:09 p.m.
Subject: Congrats on Akron

Dear Mayor Bloomberg,

Wow. I gotta admit, I didn't see that one coming. When I heard you had bought an entire U.S. city I was so shocked I nearly Rokered.* I mean, I sent out a government-wide memo instructing all branches (including my secret BFF, Chief Justice Roberts) to assist you in whatever way you needed, but never did I dream of this. Good for you.

Well, now that you've fixed the "mayor problem," let's move forward with our plan to target Santa Claus posthaste. Obesity in America is over, starting today!

Happy Thanksgiving.

B.H.O.

Michael was on Cloud Three—the highest cloud allowed since he'd banned clouds over three.

Back in the day, ol' Nanny Bloomberg got a lot of flak for telling people not to eat or smoke or drink things he didn't want them to. He rubbed a lot of people the wrong way back then, but his policies resulted in many people living longer lives—so that they could witness firsthand the Overpopulation Murder Riots of 2022.

---

* A term referencing formerly obese, formerly living weatherman Al Roker, who admitted to soiling himself during a television interview. This term is still wildly popular in 2044 and is a recognized word in the *Merriam-Bloomberg Dictionary*.

-----Original Message-----
From: Michael Bloomberg <MayorPoppins@nyc.gov>
To: Barack Obama <POTUSwiththeMOSTUS@whitehouse.gov>
Cc: Denis McDonough <DMcDonough@whitehouse.gov>
Sent: Thu, Nov 28, 2013 4:18 pm
Subject: Obesity In America

Dear Mr. President,
Thank you so much for your kind words. I have so many plans to fix the United
States! I can't wait to get started. I have so many decisions to make on behalf of our
citizens! Thank goodness those mouth-breathers have people as smart as us!

It's so awesome to own my own city. Akron is such a lame name, though. Who do I
contact about officially changing the name of the city? What do you think of this:
Bloombergberg? SO great, right?

Also, Nic Cage finally got in touch with me. Here's something learned the hard way:
Don't turn to Nic Cage to fix your problems. That guy is crazy. Not "crazy" like "man,
all girls are crazy." I'm talking crazy like "I'm going to eat rat poison and howl at the
moon" —crazy.

MAYOR Mike Bloomberg
Bloombergberg, OH

President Obama put his BlackBerry down on the seat of his work
cart and tallied up his work score with the little pencil. His handicap put
him slightly ahead of Biden—whose handicap was that he was mentally
handicapped.

Six more emails came in. All from Bloomberg. All some variation of
incredible excitement at the new obesity push, or rants about Nicolas Cage.
POTUS fired off a quick email.

-----Original Message-----
From: Barack Obama <POTUSwiththeMOSTUS@whitehouse.gov>
To: Denis McDonough <DMcDonough@whitehouse.gov>
Sent: Thu, Nov 28, 2013 10:51 pm
Subject: Oh crap

What have we done?

– Did You Know? –
The breeding of elves
and Reindeer created an
elfdeer, which was a horrible
affront to nature.

4.

SANTA THE POOR
ROLE MODEL

- Did You Know? -
John KERRY was foR
Santa Claus beforE he
was against him.

A nd so, Michael Bloomberg, who had now broken Boss Tweed's all-time record of election purchases,* was ready to turn his full attention to the obesity epidemic that threatened the very big-boned core of American society. More importantly, he was going to set his sights (which were usually aligned with normal people's knees) on Santa Claus. To Mike Bloomberg, Santa Claus was Public Enemy #1. Worse than Hitler. The Johnny Appleseed of Type 2 diabetes.

At first, the Mayors Against Fatties, which consisted of only Mayor Bloomberg but sounded better in the plural, started off small. They (he) introduced themselves (himself) to Americans with a blistering op-ed piece carried in many newspapers around the country on the strength of Bloomberg's reputation as former mayor of New York and new mayor of Akron. When he followed up with an op-ed the next day that basically said the exact same thing the papers unanimously declined to print it. Not the kind of person to take "No thank you, we printed something very similar to this yesterday" for an answer, he proceeded to buy over 250 newspapers across the country and name himself editor-in-chief. It was a huge expenditure, though he managed to take advantage of the "buy two newspapers, get one free" deals that had been available since the advent of the Internet.

Every day for four straight weeks Bloomberg's newspapers hammered Santa for being an overweight, negative influence on America's children. From the *Boston Herald-Bloomberg* to the *Cleveland Plain Bloomberger* all the way to the *San Diego Bloomberg-Tribune,* Santa was assailed as "A

---

* Source: *Guinness Book of World Records* and a Wikipedia page edited by a fourteen year old.

Propagator of Jiggliness" and "Commander in Chief of Big Bummery." Mike Bloomberg pulled no punches (mainly because years ago he had banned them).

Stuff Stockings, Not Bellies

Unhealthy Lifestyles Shouldn't be Celebrated

FAT FAT FAT FAT FAT FAT FAT FAT

DIET, EXERCISE WOULD BE THE BEST PRESENTS

Despite Bloomberg's intense, focused efforts, polls showed that the American public's opinion hadn't changed *at all* on the issue—they simply loved Santa without reservation.

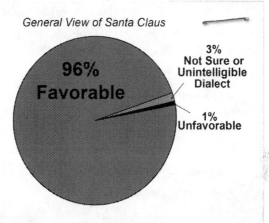

General View of Santa Claus

96%
Favorable

3%
Not Sure or
Unintelligible
Dialect

1%
Unfavorable

Source: CNN Dec. 6-9, 2013

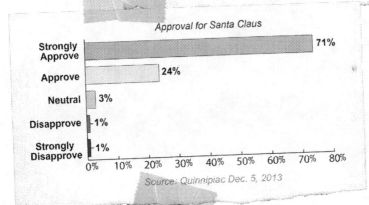

Approval for Santa Claus

Strongly Approve — 71%
Approve — 24%
Neutral — 3%
Disapprove — 1%
Strongly Disapprove — 1%

Source: Quinnipiac Dec. 5, 2013

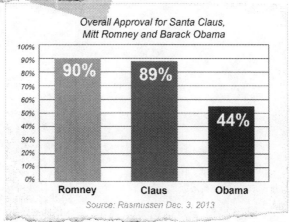

Overall Approval for Santa Claus,
Mitt Romney and Barack Obama

Romney 90%
Claus 89%
Obama 44%

Source: Rasmussen Dec. 3, 2013

More determined than ever, Bloomberg pressed on. President Obama offered him a helping hand in the form of all the writers who wrote, revised, and rewrote the memos explaining the attacks on the embassy in Benghazi. But even those seventy-five top-notch scribes couldn't make a dent in the polls.

Unsure of what he was doing wrong, he met with publishing legend S. I. Newhouse to get his advice. It was then that Bloomberg learned something stunning: Americans don't read. Turns out that the newspaper's primary purpose in the twenty-first century was to line birdcages.*

A day after meeting with Newhouse there were 250 unexplained simultaneous newspaper fires throughout the country. After the insurance payouts, Bloomberg had turned a nifty profit, which he dedicated to manipulating other forms of media to his advantage. And he hit every conceivable platform to get his message across. Here are just a few examples from the "Ho Ho Ho-besity Is No Laughing Matter" series:

– Did You Know? –
Cupid the Reindeer's mother was struck on Highway 12 by Matthew Broderick.

* Source: The Internet.

Hang In There? Not If You're Too Fat.

Million Mayors Against Fatties

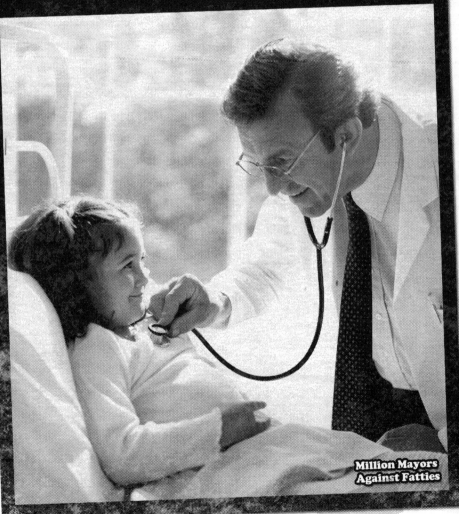

Yes, Virginia,
You Have Type 2 Diabetes.

Million Mayors
Against Fatties

"Thin Is 'In'" TV PSA

By Mayor Michael Bloomberg

OPEN ON: A room full of 100 gorgeous thin models. No fat Kates, like Upton or Winslet. Just thin ones like Moss. All wear two-piece bikinis.

Kate Moss: Hello, I'm Kate Moss, and I'm here with a bunch of my normal friends to talk to you about the importance of staying thin. I've spent most of my life in all sorts of great places—exotic beaches, incredible seafood restaurants, and Johnny Depp's bedroom. What do all three of those places have in common?

Brooke Burke: They're all places where you can get crabs.

Everyone laughs.

Naomi Campbell: True, but they're also all places that are only accessible if you're thin. Johnny Depp won't kick you out of bed for eating crackers, but he will if you eat Marshmallow Fluff. Just ask Sherilyn Fenn.

Everyone laughs.

Bar Refaeli: Or if you steal his jewelry. Just ask Winona Ryder.

Everyone laughs.

Gisele Bundchen: But being fat is no laughing matter. Did you know that being overweight means you're one hundred thousand times more likely to wind up living in a trailer park and taking vacations at the Mall of America than if you're thin like us?

Bar Refaeli: Being fat like, say, Santa Claus can lead to health problems, happiness problems, and sexual dysfunction. Literally everyone in this room has had sex with either Leonardo DiCaprio or Derek Jeter.

Everyone: Or both.

Bar Refaeli: But none of us have been with Santa. Don't you want to be cool like us?

Naomi Campbell: I may be incredibly unpleasant, but men are attracted to me because I'm thin. If you're overweight, you'll likely wind up with someone like this:

(continues)

Holds up picture of Chaz Bono. Everyone gasps.

Kate Moss: You know what's sexy? Being thin enough to count your ribs—not eating a plate of ribs like a big fat pig.

Bar Refaeli: So watch your weight and have a happy life. Don't let the Santa Clauses of the world set a bad example that leads you to a life of being average.

I walk onstage. Everyone squeals like I'm a member of the Beatles.

Mayor Bloomberg: I'm Mayor Bloomberg, and I paid for this message with money I found in between the seat cushions of my couch.

All the girls applaud me and try to kiss me and stuff. The Mayors Against Fatties logo comes up, and maybe a strike-through of Santa Claus.

THE END.

If you're reading this past 8 p.m. PLEASE GO TO BED.

Mayor Bloomberg's director's chair.

Craft services table.

Naomi Campbell's dressing room.

When you eat ALONE
you eat with Santa!
Join a
Food-Sharing Club
TODAY!

Bloomberg's anti-Santa jihad continued unabated. Though it still didn't have the impact he was hoping, he did begin to make waves.

You probably already know this but on February 25, 2020 a blimp carrying Michael Bloomberg, Donald Trump, Charlie Sheen, and every Kardashian caught fire and burned at a landing strip in New Jersey. It was exactly like the *Hindenburg* disaster except it wasn't a hydrogen blimp and it wasn't a disaster.

On April 13, 2014, statistics wunderkind Nate Silver launched a new website, santapopularity.com, with the aim of its becoming the most accurate Santa statistics website in the world. Why is anyone's guess, but it certainly works well with this book's storyline.

Santapopulartity.com showed Santa with an approval rating of 78 percent, an all-time low for the most popular, most charitable man in history. Karl Rove, who had just begun an internship at the site to learn how numbers work, and who knows a thing or two about attack ads, called the results significant. "I hate this administration. I hate Michael Bloomberg. I hate flowers and sunshine and the sound of laughter. And I look like a bullfrog that someone put a pair of glasses on in the hopes of taking a funny Instagram. But damn, I admire the work that has been done to discredit Santa Claus. I don't know why it's being done, but it is being done *well*. Kudos."

The president's plan was working. America had begun, ever so slightly, to turn on Santa Claus. But this was not a time to rest on one's laurels (or as Joe Biden called them, "leaf sweatbands"). At 78 percent they still had their work cut out for them.

What better day to do that than the day when Americans were at their grumpiest? Fortunately that day was right around the corner: April 15.

Tax Day (also known by Timothy Geithner and much of Congress as "Honest Mistake Day").

- Did You Know? -
Until the advent of
computers, the "naughty
oR nice list" was kept on
thousands of cocktail napkins
shoved in santa's pockets.

5.

SANTA THE
TAX EVADER

- Did you know? -
Oftentimes the silence of the
North Pole is pierced by the
screams of the White Walkers.

- Did you know? -
Santa was so upset at his portrayal
in 1960s animated television specials
that he put a lump of coal in Burl
Ives's stocking and threw it at him.

"It's easier for a man with no hands to read Braille
than it is to read the United States tax code."
—Helen Keller, June 1955, a quote she may have
thought. How would we ever know, really?

"Hey, we're U.S. senators—let's sit down
and make the tax code simpler."
—No one, 1991–2014

One night before bed, Michelle turned to Barack and asked, in as sultry a voice as she could muster, "What's your favorite day of the year?"*

Now, Barack is no dummy. He knew the only correct answer was "The day we got married." He knew that all he had to say were those words, and he'd be in like Flynn. He might even get a terrorist fist bump before lights-out.

"Barack!" said his brain. "Just say those words! It's all you have to do!"

So he looked deep into Michelle's eyes, smiled warmly, and answered truthfully.

"April fifteenth."

He couldn't resist! He loved Tax Day so much! The poor guy just couldn't lie. Michelle's eyes turned cold and black—like Hitler's eyes. Barack knew he was in the doghouse and that his nookie embargo was going to last longer than Strom Thurmond's political career. That night he slept on the floor.

---

* The recounting of this personal conversation, and many like it through the book, was provided by conservative firebrand Michelle Limbaugh, formerly Michelle Obama, who renounced her liberalism when she became Rush Limbaugh's seventh (and later ninth) wife.

Every morning for six years the president would wake up super early on Tax Day, run downstairs to the Oval Office, log on to Amazon, and start buying billions of dollars of crap that the country didn't need. "This money isn't going to spend itself" was his favorite expression on Tax Day. But in 2014, it was even more special than usual.

To understand what happened on Tax Day in 2014, we must first look at what happened in June 2013 during a secret meeting between President Obama and the acting head of the IRS, Daniel Werfel. What follows is an excerpt from Mr. Werfel's diary of his experience from that time. And before you get all weird about reading someone else's diary, ask yourself why someone would write down all their thoughts and feelings if they didn't secretly want someone to read it. I meant that the day I said it to my wife when she caught me reading her journal and emails, and I mean it now.

June 5, 2013
Dear Diary,
As if things in my life couldn't get crazier, President Obama asked me to come to the White House for a secret meeting last night at 2 a.m.!!! To keep this meeting completely "off the books," I was instructed to tell no one, "not even my diary if I keep one." (I'm not going to keep any secrets from you, Diary — it's not like anyone will ever read you, because you're labeled private and no one is that big of an a-hole.) Even weirder, I'm not to go directly to the White House, but rather am supposed to use a series of secret underground tunnels that JFK installed for Marilyn and his other comfort girls.
    I arrived at the Lincoln Memorial at around 1 a.m. and walked directly to the statue of our 16th president. Thanks to the sequester there were no guards around, so no one was there to hear me utter the secret phrase:

"Ask not what your country can do for you, ask what you can do for your country" (said in a sleazy way). Suddenly a secret door opened from what appeared to be smooth marble and, moments later, I was underground, walking in a secret underground corridor toward the White House.

In that half-hour walk I saw some of the craziest things I have ever seen in my life:

* A skeleton in a suit and tie stuffed inside an old suitcase. It had a wallet with a driver's license belonging to one Vince Foster, who must've been buried alive based on all of the scratch marks on the inside of the chest. I took a picture with my cell phone just for the heck of it.

* A musty old room with a ratty old mattress on the floor and a ton of what I can only describe as "sex paraphernalia." Carved into the wall was a heart with "Nancy-n-Frank 4Ever" on the inside. Nice to see young love memorialized like that.

* A wall, much like the one at the Vietnam Veterans Memorial, with the names of all the prostitutes who serviced President Kennedy. Hard to say which wall has more names on it.

* A fancy-looking plaque on a wall that read "Jimmy Carter's Successes as President." The plaque was completely empty. Obviously.

* Jimmy Carter. He was building houses for the rats.

Finally, I made it to a door that led me out into the Rose Kennedy Garden, designed to reflect and honor the legacy of the woman who pooped out so many Kennedys. Sadly it is a garden of death and despair that resembles the land of Mordor from the Lord of the Rings trilogy. There are more ghosts in that tiny garden than in the battlefields of Europe. My skin went cold standing there and I could feel myself getting sucked into another plane of existence. I could hear assassins' bullets and airplane crashes and the screams of innocent women. Right before I slipped into unconsciousness the ghost of Lyndon Johnson visited me and told me exactly how he had had President Kennedy killed. It was horrible, yet brilliant. . . .

I came to in the arms of a Secret Service agent as he carried me toward the Rose Garden. The Rose Garden was designed to reflect and honor just roses, so it was much nicer. "We almost lost you," said the man, who smelled vaguely of a Colombian lady I had once known. "The president is waiting for you."

President Obama was standing alone in the Rose Garden, ankle deep in a pile of cigarette butts. "Thanks for coming, Daniel. With all of the negative attention the IRS is getting lately with these vicious attacks against conservatives, I thought it might be a good idea to take some of the heat off the organization and cast you folks in a positive light."

"By reforming the tax code? A flat tax sort of thing?"

The president laughed for a long time. "No. By auditing Santa Claus." He saw my stunned expression. "Now, before you say anything, I want to assure you that I have a plan in place that will have ol' St. Nick's popularity down by Tax Day 2014, so you're going to come out looking much more like a hero than a bully."

"Why . . . would we have anything to do with Santa Claus? How is that in our jurisdiction?"

"Daniel, he runs a small business that, admittedly, does not originate in the United States, but it does operate in the United States for a significant part of the year."

"But he gives toys away. What is there to audit?" I stammered.

"Sure, maybe that is what he winds up doing with his product, but I've already investigated the list of our country's tax-exempt organizations, which I have on my desk for many reasons," he chuckled, and then gave me a weird wink that somehow felt sleazy. "And he's not on that list.* So if he's not tax-exempt, and he operates a business, then he needs to pay his fair share. We can no

---

* The list included Freedom for Liberty Foundation, the Freedom Society, American Association for Freedom, Freedom Lovers, Hooray for Freedom, and Freedom Freedom Freedom.

longer afford to coddle the top one percent at the expense of the middle class. You know, blah blah blah, we are the ninety-nine percent yadda yadda et cetera. All that stuff. Did I say 'fair share' and 'one percent' yet? I think we've got something; don't you agree, Eric?"

Suddenly, Eric Holder emerged from the shadows. Dressed in a black ninja suit, he and his almost Hitler mustache completely blended into the night.

"That's right, Mr. President. Legally you're on solid footing. He manufactures so much product that he certainly owes American a great deal in taxes, back taxes, penalties, and late fees. Why should he be exempt? He's not General Electric or the NFL. Santa's tax bill will be a windfall."

"Think of all that money we can turn around and spend," said the president, a touch of drool falling from the lower right corner of his mouth.

"Sir, why is the attorney general here?"

"If I may, Mr. President?" Eric Holder asked. Obama nodded. "To be honest, this administration is breaking the law on an hourly basis lately —"

"Not to mention ignoring the Constitution," the president added with a laugh. "Remember, I'm a —"

"Constitutional scholar, I know," Holder replied, the tiniest hint of exasperation in his voice. "Anyway, we're breaking enough laws that I felt it was best that I not leave the president's side for the next few months. He basically needs round-the-clock legal counsel. I'm sorry if I startled you."

"No, I'm glad you're here," I said honestly. "It's good to know that we're in the clear . . . to begin auditing Santa Claus." I couldn't believe I had just said that out loud.

"Great! Now we have one other matter to discuss," said Obama. "I'm worried about this whole business with the IRS and conservative groups. I want to make absolutely sure that you have enough assets to keep up the good work."

"Absolutely," I replied. "We'll make life hell for anyone who dared vote against you."

"Amen," said Obama. A quiet set over the group. The president looked around. "That's what we people of Christian faith would say at that point, right?"

"Yes, sir."

"Good. Amen. So, who are you going after next? Amen."

"A TV network called TheBlaze —"

"What is that, some sort of gay rights network? Now that it's politically convenient, I'm a big supporter of gay marriage, so we can't —"

"No, sir, it's not a gay rights network."

"A magazine for retired firefighters? That seems weird. Did you know that Mitt Romney wanted to fire teachers, police officers, and firefighters?"

"No, sir. It's a . . . news network, I guess, for lack of a better term. It's owned by Glenn Beck."

The night went completely still. A rose tree near where I was standing wilted and died right before my eyes.

"Glenn Beck?" the president spat out. "Divert all resources into destroying 'TheBlaze.'"

"The truth lives there," I volunteered.

"That," the president said ominously, "is what I'm afraid of." He and Holder looked at each other. They were afraid. "You know what you have to do. Good night, and good luck."

"Thank you, Mr. President."

"No, no, Good Night and Good Luck. Have you seen it?"

"No," I said.

"It was a movie about a journalist doing his job. Scariest movie I ever saw. Terrifying. One final question while I have you, Daniel. Can I write off my new set of golf clubs if I used them to play golf with John Boehner and we discussed business?"

"That's a definite red flag, Mr. President. I wouldn't."

"That's what I thought. Eric, write up an executive order to fix this and I'll sign it in the morning." The attorney general nodded and disappeared into the night.

The president turned his back to me, and as I headed off I saw him light three cigarettes and begin smoking them all at the same time. Here was a man who was getting stuff done.

Did you know that the Payroll Withholding Tax was a temporary measure that was introduced just over one hundred years ago, in 1943? It was just supposed to help the United States get through World War II, but they liked it so much they kept it through World Wars III, IV, and V!

Immediately afterward, Santa was sent an IRS questionnaire.

INTERNAL REVENUE SERVICE

To Whom It May Concern: Please fill out this questionnaire so that we may better understand your business. Failure to do so may result in further action on our behalf.

Approximate time to complete this questionnaire: 45–90 days.

What was the annual income of your company last year? _____

What was your company's profit or loss last year?_____

How many employees does your company have?_____

Who are the primary investors in your company? _____

Does your company, the directors of your company, or anyone associated with your company maintain funds offshore? _____

How much real estate do you own? _____

List any mortgages against that property. _____

Has anyone in your company committed a misdemeanor or had a dream? _____

Who, What, Where, When, Why?_____

Please list anyone you've ever done business with in any way, shape, or form. _____

_____

Page (1)

92 pages later. . .

INTERNAL REVENUE SERVICE

Where were you when John F. Kennedy was assassinated? _____

Have you seen *The Sixth Sense*? If so, did you see the
ending coming? If so, what tipped you off? _____

Do you believe Bruce Willis's wife really would've shown up at that
restaurant on their anniversary knowing her husband was dead? _____

Do you think it would be awesome if the Death Star were real? _____

List and summarize the books you have read in the last three years. Put
the list in alphabetical order based on the 803rd letter in the first chapter
of each book. _____

_____

Without looking, write down the names of as many Beatles songs as
you can. Take that list to a local bakery and see if they'll trade it for a
cinnamon bun. _____

_____

If you shot the sheriff but did not shoot the deputy, are you still a bad
guy? What if the sheriff was laundering money via a "magical" operation
that seemingly had no revenue and incurred no expenses? _____

Tape a banana to your head, sing a stupid song, and make a YouTube
video that achieves 18 million hits or more.

Page (93)

The Elf tasked with handling mail that day drew smiley faces on the
survey and returned it to the IRS. They were not amused.

With a ten-month head start, the IRS was able to secretly investigate
Santa and, in conjunction with the Justice Department, build an extensive

and airtight case to present to the American people, and that's exactly what they did— just in time to make the morning news on Tax Day.

And so the government had successfully launched Phase II of its plan to bring down Santa Claus. And the IRS audit scheme, which had seemed improbable at best that June evening in the Rose Garden, resonated with an American public that was angry to seemingly pay more taxes than those who "should." Namely, Santa Claus.

PARTIAL TRANSCRIPT

[TODAY SHOW]
[Tape # 26652-9]
[Airdate–04/15/2014]

Al Roker: So, make sure you bring your umbrellas on the East Coast. Matt?

Matt Lauer: Thanks, Al. (Turns to new co-host Lara Logan) How are you enjoying your first day on the job so far, Lara?

Lara Logan: I'm having a blast, Matt, thank you. And thank you for pushing Savannah Guthrie under the bus to open up the position for me.

Matt: My pleasure! Actually, just to clarify, I threw Ann Curry under the bus. I pushed Savannah in front of a bus.

Lara: What???

Matt: Yep! If people are going to cast me as the villain now, I might as well play the role.

Al: This makes me very uncomfortable —

Matt: SHUT UP, FAT MAN, OR YOU'RE NEXT! I'LL PULL THE STAPLE FROM YOUR STOMACH AND USE IT TO STAPLE YOUR MOUTH SHUT! Now, Lara, you have an interesting story coming out of Washington this morning.

Lara: . . . That's right, Matt. (clears throat) The IRS is on everyone's mind lately, from continued fallout from last year's scandal to the fact that today is dreaded Tax Day. But the IRS is also on the mind of someone rather unexpected — Santa Claus. That's because the IRS has launched a comprehensive investigation into the North Pole operation of Santa, claiming that The Jolly One owes hundreds of millions of dollars in back taxes.

CUT TO: PRESS CONFERENCE FOOTAGE OF
IRS LAWYER MAKING STATEMENT.

Lawyer: We believe Santa Claus has long been in gross violation of US tax law and we intend to recoup that which is rightfully the American people's. It is important to send the message that everyone must pay their fair share of taxes and that no one is above the law. Not even the one percent. And fat cats like Santa, literally super fat as we've heard so much about lately, must actually pay more than their fair share in order to help out average Americans. I don't want to dictate policy, but let me say that rich people like Santa should pay more in taxes, to say nothing of not sheltering their money offshore in places like the Cayman Islands or the North Pole. So please, just know that your government is working to protect you. Thank you.

CUT BACK TO: LIVE: THE TODAY SHOW SET. A frantic stagehand is dragging Lara Logan's body off the stage.

Stagehand (In between sobs): She's been poisoned.

Matt: Sounds like the work of Vladimir Putin to me!

Al: What? Why —

Matt: I'm just kidding. It was me. I'd like to welcome my brand brand new co-host, Soledad O'Brien.

(Soledad O'Brien hesitantly walks onto the set.)

Soledad: I don't want to be here.

Matt: Don't forget, next week is another installment of "Where In The World Is Matt Lauer!"

Al: I'm guessing Attica.

Matt: Wrong! The answer is no one cares anymore! We'll be right back.

Police officer: Mr. Lauer, may I speak with you for a moment —

Matt: You'll never take me alive!

Static. End of transmission.

OP-ED PAGE
We Know When You've Been Naughty!

by Robert Mantooth

Something doesn't add up. That's the opinion of a few number crunchers at the IRS, according to a recently leaked document. It appears they're having a hard time reconciling how one particular North Pole-based company can deliver gifts galore to boys and girls around the world without ever having made a profit! And before you say "magic" remember: the intrepid agents have already heard every excuse in the world. Sources say it's especially hard to determine if the books have been cooked because there aren't any books to cook! It shouldn't take a rocket scientist (or a forensic accountant, for that matter) to figure out that someone must be stuffing their stockings because no one in their right mind is going to invest in a company that puts smiles over profit! We say: it's high time the government make a list and check it multiple times until they've closed all tax loopholes and taken action against the scofflaws!

SPORTS FINAL

Mostly sunny, 55/44. Thursday, April 17, 2014

DAILY◉NEWS

SANTA CLAUS AND I SHOULD PAY MORE: WARREN BUFFETT

SEE PAGES 4-5

- Did you know? -
Santa often tells friends he's "Buddhist"
because he thinks it "sounds cool."

6.

SANTA THE
POLLUTER

- Did you know? -
It really bothers Santa
that stores start with the
christmas music crap the day
after Halloween.

Vice President Biden was on his hands and knees, rummaging through the scrub near the eleventh hole of the work course.

"Give it up, Joe," said the president. "You're not going to find it."

"Awww, man," grumbled Biden, "that's like the fiftieth one today. I'm polluting the place with work balls."

At that moment, the president had an epiphany. It was one of the greatest epiphanies he'd had in some time. Definitely in the top five.

The epiphany the president was currently experiencing was sparked by Biden's mention of pollution. Everyone knew pollution was bad. No one of any political persuasion could be "for" pollution—that's crazy!

"Joe?" asked the president, as he lined up his seven-iron on the work ball.

"Yeah, boss?" asked the vice president as he rifled through a small shrub.

My Top 5 Epiphanies

1. Reverend Wright makes me look bad!

2. My voting base likes cool colors and simple words!

3. I don't know what I'm doing!

4. I'd better put off implementing MeCare until after the 2014 midterms!

5. This epiphany!

"What'd you get for Christmas last year?"

"Coal, boss."

"And the year before that?"

"Coal."

And all throughout your childhood?"

"Coal, boss. Coal."

"And do you remember the speech I gave a few weeks ago? The one where I said we needed to get away from coal because it's dirty and it causes pollution? Coal. Pollution. Coal. Pollution. And someone we know flies around leaving coal all over the place. Spreading coal. Spreading pollution. Following me?"

Biden stopped his search and stood up. He looked at the president and smiled. He was trying real hard to put two and two together. The president could see it in his eyes. Barack waited, watching Joe's face as the poor guy struggled to comprehend what the president had said. Struggled to piece the words together and spark some kind of electrical impulse in his brain that might result in the response the president was hoping for.

Barack smiled. "I'll just tell—"

"No! I can do this, boss!" Joe said. The president waited. Joe's eyes lit up, and then shut down, lit up, shut down. Barack was very patient with Joe, but he really wanted to get back to work.

"Santa Claus, man," said the president.

"Santa Claus, man," Joe said a solid three seconds after the president. "It's so funny that we said that at the same time."

In short order they came up with talking points that soon made their way into the media outlets:

Santa Claus was the tip of what they declared to be a gigantic, filthy, horrible, terrible, threatening coal iceberg. Santa Claus, in no uncertain terms, was a major polluter.

By flying around and leaving these lumps of coal in children's stockings, Santa was creating a major disposal problem. The scope and size of the problem was unknown but clearly had to be significant—there was no shortage of naughty children. In fact, they argued, the number of naughty children had risen dramatically since the late 1970s. No one knows why.

Those lumps of coal added up, they said, and eventually found their way into landfills or were tossed angrily by naughty nonrecipients of gifts into backyards across the country. Given enough time those lumps of coal could accumulate and create an eyesore, taint water supplies, trip an emu, or spontaneously burst into flames and spark a forest fire. It was an environmental catastrophe in the making. Something obviously had to be done and the government was just the doer to do that something.

Not to mention the fact that due to Santa's mysterious nature, the actual origin of his coal was not known. Was it what's known as "clean" coal?

Did he have a mining operation in place to acquire the coal? Where was his mining operation located? Were his mines up to code? Who worked the mines? Children? What were they paid? Were they unionized? And if he was forcing children to work in mines without a union, were they at least getting all major holidays off?

Too many questions and too few answers.

On January 14, 2014, the United States Environmental Protection Agency began the process of investigating Santa's impact on the environment. It started, as it often did, with a series of emails.

To: Curtis Pearce <c.pearce@epa.gov>
From: Michael McDermott <m.mcdermott@epa.gov>
Sent: Fri, Jan 3, 2014 09:17 am
Subject: Party!

Matt!
Had a great time at your NYE party. Booyah! You guys really know how to entertain. Donna was RUINED. She slept for two days afterwards LOL!
Curt

To: Michael McDermott <m.mcdermott@epa.gov>
From: Curtis Pearce <c.pearce@epa.gov>
Sent: Fri, Jan 3, 2014 09:32 am
Subject: Re: Party!

Curt was that email meant for me? Confused.

To: Curtis Pearce <c.pearce@epa.gov>
From: Michael McDermott <m.mcdermott@epa.gov>
Sent: Fri, Jan 3, 2014 09:44 am
Subject: Report

Ha! Sorry. That was for my bud Matt. That auto-address feature always gets me. LOL!

DOJ has asked me to put together a standard exploratory report about the environmental impact of the coal distributed by Santa Claus. Nothing major. I want to bring your team in on this because I know you've been looking for something since you wrapped up the study on cow farts.
Curt

To: Michael McDermott <m.mcdermott@epa.gov>
From: Curtis Pearce <c.pearce@epa.gov>
Sent: Fri, Jan 3, 2014 10:17 am
Subject: Re: Report

Hi Curt -
It was an Impact Study on Rural Bovine Methane Emissions. I think "cow farts" trivializes what took up thousands of man-hours and cost me my marriage.
I'll get the team on it immediately.
Michael

Now, if there's one thing that bureaucrats do well* it's generate reports. When compiling reports, not only do bureaucrats leave no stone unturned; they also write reports about having left no stone unturned, the odds of turning stones in the future, and the impact of turned stones on indigenous insects, animals, and peoples. One of those reports went so far as to suggest that indigenous peoples would not notice a stone, turned or unturned, because they were far too busy operating a very lucrative casino and were unlikely to be meandering about the woods looking for jostled stones.

But we digress. Back to the EPA.

In short order, what started off as a simple email had blossomed into more pages than you could shake a stick at. And you couldn't shake a stick at it, because there were barely any trees left after it was printed. Copies were then sent to the Department of Justice, every member of Congress, numerous media sources, and of course the executive branch:

Honorable Barack Obama
c/o The White House
1600 Pennsylvania Avenue
N.W. Washington, D.C. 20500

Dear Mr. President:
   I am pleased to deliver to you the Report to Congress on the Long-Term Impact of Stocking-Delivered Coal. The report contains results from several studies conducted pursuant to the Resource Conservation and Recovery Act of 1976.
   The assessment details our findings regarding coal delivered to domestic stockings and the subsequent storage and disposal of coal and its potential impact to the environment. The report also offers proposed solutions for any potential problems.
   The reports and appendices total 1,522 pages and are spread into four volumes for your convenience.

Sincerely,

C. S. Pearce

Curtis S. Pearce
Director

---

* There is, in fact, *only* one thing bureaucrats do well: generate reports.

The report served as glowing testimony to the ability of governmental agencies to assemble large clusters of words and have them printed at great expense. It also served as a scathing indictment of the previously ignored coal distribution policies of Mr. Santa Claus. In the bureaucratic world the 1,522-page report was considered a masterpiece and in fact went on to win *Best Really Big Report* in the 2015 Bureaucratic Awards—which are like the Oscars, but no one is hotter than a 6.

THE UNITED STATES OF AMERICA
2015 BUREAUCRATIC AWARDS

Hosted by Tom Bergeron

Program:

Best Unread Monstrosity

Affordable Care Act (a.k.a. Obamacare)

Least Use of Valid Words

Stat of Edracation in Amerca

Longest Time to Produce Something

TSA Report on Cancer-Scanners

Best Really Big Report

Report to Congress on the Long Term Impact of Stocking-Delivered Coal

You are cordially invited

Of course, the difficulty of translating Bureaucratese into English ensured that only roughly 18 percent of the book was comprehensible by a layman. And 19 percent of the book was comprehensible by a laywoman. It's perfectly okay to point out when a laywoman does something better than a layman, but never vice versa.

– Did you know? –
Santa made up the mistletoe rule just to kiss ladies.

Some of the highlights of this remarkably comprehensive work were:

(p.117)
"...By virtue of having received coal in his or her stocking, the child is presumed to be 'naughty' and therefore can not be trusted to properly dispose of the coal. Our findings show that naughty children often throw the coal at local nerds which, while funny, presents a complex pollution problem in cities, suburbs and rural areas where naughty children habitate."

(p.323)
"...Although inconclusive, the data suggest that in households where perpetually naughty children reside, the annual acquisition of coal could lead up to hazardous buildup of coal residue and dust over time. Naturally this presents health concerns, in particular for children in the same household who are not naughty yet exposed to the potentially detrimental elements of the naughty child's coal.

(p.555)
"Some tests conclude that perpetually naughty children could receive lethal doses of coal dust by age 182."

(p.876)
"Suggested alternatives to coal include locally-derived rocks, bark and organic wheatgrass, which the naughty child could consume and convert to energy."

(p.877)
"Nuclear is not a viable alternative for naughty children, despite our firm belief that the United Nations could sanction kids effectively."

(p.1034)
"No correlation was found between coal distribution and continental drift."

(p.1328)
"This page intentionally left blank."

It was a helluva read to anyone who read it, though no one really read it. Most folks skimmed or settled for summaries, picked out words they liked, or let TV pundits and Facebook comment threads do the heavy lifting for them. Once the facts were kind of absorbed or assumed it didn't take long before a slow news day caused the media to sit up and take notice.

As you would imagine, the threat of a morbidly obese stranger flying around and exposing defenseless children to poison struck a raw nerve. It became the talk of the town, so to speak, the town being all the United States and a lot of Canada (what else are they going to talk about while in line for eight hours to see a doctor?).

OWN

WORRIED FOR MY KIDS

HARDBALL WITH CHRIS MATTHEWS

XMESS TIME

MSNBC

4:35 EST

PANEL ON THE CYCLE AGREES NO ONE WATCHING

LIVE

BUCK SEXTON

SANTA WORKING FOR CHINA?

THE BLAZE

THE TRUTH LIVES HERE   THE TRUTH LIVES HERE   THE TRUTH LIVES HERE

LIVE

5:22 PM CT

In the age of Tumblr and Twitter and Facebook, but probably not LinkedIn, it didn't take long for the story to spread like wildfire. A group of men with little to no prospect of ever kissing a girl formed the *Coal Truth* movement, dedicated to exposing the government's involvement in the coal conspiracy. They didn't have much in the way of facts to stand on but that didn't stop them from having 189,422 likes on Facebook.*

In 2013, Facebook was a handy way to spread facts and misinformation. But mostly misinformation. Those not smart enough to resist commenting could easily find themselves in the midst of an unpleasant war of words, with fearless netizens using their keyboards to bravely insult and threaten people who were hundreds if not thousands of miles away.

David Liss   My God people, it's a lump of coal. Lighten up!
16 hours ago

Beth Miller   Typical republitard denying reality. FYI IRAQ HAD NO WMD.
15 hours ago

David Liss   Talking about coal being harmless. Not Iraq.
15 hours ago

Beth Miller   says the moron who voted for Bushitler!
15 hours ago

David Liss   I didn't vote because I hated both candidates.
15 hours ago

Beth Miller   BUSH STOLE THE ELECTION.
15 hours ago

Katie Dougherty   Shut your democrap mouth and O'Bummer sucks!
14 hours ago

Todd Washburn   David's right. It's just a lump of coal not armageddon.
14 hours ago

Christine Bostick   Just coal? Lemme guess ur the type who would destroy Alaska for oil.
14 hours ago

Benjamin Korman   Hey, guys, the original message on this thread was "Happy Birthday, Ben." Not sure how we got here.
8 hours ago

Beth Miller   Shut up, Ben.
8 hours ago

---

* Facebook is a multibillion-dollar birthday reminder machine.

Peanuts, trans-fats, hyper kids, bicycle helmets, seat belts—these are things that we once gave no thought to. And so it was with coal in the stocking. Alas, when something that's been unquestioned for so long finds itself in the spotlight being questioned, things can get rough pretty quick—just ask Muammar Qaddafi. A scared, outraged, and largely uninformed public wanted answers. Santa was soon called to the carpet and forced to defend his policy. Lacking the proper public relations savvy and not having the guidance of a PR professional, Santa made one of the biggest blunders of his career. He appeared on *Piers Morgan*.

CNN

*** CNN/PIERS MORGAN TRANSCRIPT ***

PIERS: BUT TELL ME WHY YOU NEED THE COAL.

SANTA: BECAUSE THAT'S THE WAY WE'VE ALWAYS DONE IT.

PIERS: SO YOUR ARGUMENT IS THAT'S HOW IT'S DONE, SO I'LL JUST KEEP POLLUTING.

SANTA: IT'S NOT POLLUTING.

PIERS: REALLY? YOU'RE LEAVING COAL ALL OVER THE PLACE AND THAT'S NOT POLLUTING?

SANTA: IT SENDS A MESSAGE TO NAUGHTY KIDS.

PIERS: THAT SANTA WILL POLLUTE THE EARTH IF THEY DON'T LIVE UP TO YOUR EXPECTATIONS?

SANTA: NO! JUST THAT THEY SHOULD BE NICE OR THEY GET A LUMP OF COAL.

PIERS: POISONED.

SANTA: IT'S NOT POISON. IT'S COAL.

PIERS: AND WHAT HAPPENS WHEN THEY BURN IT?

SANTA: THEY DON'T BURN IT.

PIERS: AND YOU KNOW THIS HOW?

SANTA: WELL, MOST KIDS AREN'T GOING TO BURN IT.

PIERS: MOST. OKAY, BUT SOME MAY?

SANTA: I DON'T SEE WHY THEY WOULD.

PIERS: IF THEY HAVE A STEAM ENGINE TRAIN THEY MIGHT.

SANTA: WHY WOULD A CHILD --

PIERS: THE SECOND AMENDMENT IS ANTIQUATED, DON'T YOU THINK?

SANTA: IS THERE SOMETHING WRONG WITH YOU?

- Did you know? -
Ted Kennedy killed a lady.

> Funny, even way back then they were trying to
> switch from coal. And I think we will someday.
> They keep telling us that solar is right around
> the corner once they get the technology right.
> I remember the 2030 New York Car Show debuted a
> Chevrofiat Solyndrive solar-powered vehicle. You
> could go thirty miles with only eight battery
> changes! But the best part was the feeling of
> excitement you'd get when you turned the engine
> on. You'd slowly insert the key, turn it clockwise,
> and think, "Is this thing going to blow up?" Love
> that adrenaline rush you get
> from driving!

By now, the damage was done. The public perception of stocking coal had been totally altered. Like the food ingredient MSG it had gone from being ubiquitous and accepted to being a total pariah. It didn't take too long before others jumped on the bandwagon.

COMEDIENNE-TURNED-SCIENTIST JENNY McCARTHY: "COAL CAUSES AUTISM"

Critics Site Troubles for Some Energy Producers/Manufacturers

VOL. 32 NO.10

THURSDAY OCTOBER

Santa Claus promised to cease using coal as a method of punishing those he considered naughty. Instead he and the elves would investigate acceptable, sustainable, biodegradable alternatives. The Report to Congress on the Long-Term Impact of Stocking-Delivered Coal did more than just end Santa's coal policy, however; it did one other thing that reports tend to do: It sent other like-minded bureaucrats scurrying to generate even more reports.

IMPACT OF JINGLING BELLS ON GEESE MIGRATION

FLYING CARIBOU FLATULENCE AND THE OZONE LAYER

OPEN CHIMNEYS AND GLOBAL WARMING

TOY WORKSHOP EMISSIONS IN THE ARTIC CIRCLE

UNITED NATIONS REPORT ON THE MASSACRE OF PINE TREES

According to the Government Accountability Office's annual Report on Reports, the initial report on stocking coal and the reports that resulted from that initial report were responsible for the deforestation of 18 percent of Brazil's natural rain forest.

The effort to raise awareness of the threat of coal lumps, if there was a threat, spawned an unfortunate new bureaucracy that green-lit several regrettable public service ad campaigns.

LUMPY THE LUMP
OF COAL SAYS,

"DON'T THROW ME AWAY!"

If you come into possession of a lump of coal, don't throw it away! Call your local sanitation officials and ask them for the proper way to discard your unwanted lumps. Remember, don't lump it in with your household trash! Get it?

THIS NATIVE
AMERICAN
IS CRYING
BECAUSE
YOU STOLE
AMERICA AND
POISONED
IT WITH
COAL LUMPS.

U.S. DEPARTMENT OF
COAL LUMP AWARENESS

YES WE CANNOT
DUMP THAT LUMP

7.

SANTA THE
ANIMAL ABUSER

- Did you know? -
Santa has a Pink Floyd
tattoo he'd Rather not
talk about.

Back in Washington, the Obama administration was energized by its success. It was such a rare occurrence to succeed that they didn't quite know how to celebrate, much like when the Washington Generals finally beat the Harlem Globetrotters and then entered into a suicide pact.

Despite their success, the administration knew that in order for this anti-Santa revolution to really take hold, it needed a grassroots element. White House officials were constantly on the lookout for populist issues to rile up the nation, and for citizens to fight for these issues on their behalf. They found the perfect combination of issue and soldier in an area once described by Hugo Chavez as "too socialist for my liking": Vermont.

The U.S. Department of Watching People had been watching Brandon Plauser for months, and he was perfect. Brandon studied Native American Feminist History at a rural college in Vermont. When not writing long papers about the struggles of Native American women in a patriarchal, pre-industrial, field-dwelling society, he had some time to pursue other causes. One of those causes, getting Brandon Plauser a girlfriend, proved to be very difficult. Fortunately, the other cause, promoting animal rights, was much easier. Like many college sophomores, Brandon took his passion for animal rights activism to the extreme. He was a vegan, though he felt that veganism didn't go far enough. Brandon refused to eat any vegetable that came from a farm, because the manure used to enrich the soil may have once been an animal before it was excrement (or "a brown corpse," as Brandon called it, often taking time to give a proper burial and funeral to feces he found lying about). Brandon also believed that all animals should be free to roam as they saw fit, unburdened by a leash, so he would walk around campus "liberating" dogs that had been tied up by their owners.*

---

* It might be sheer coincidence, but statistics show a tremendous increase in dogs being struck by cars in areas where Brandon lives.

Another favorite hobby of Brandon's was to harass fellow students as they ate their meatloaf in the school cafeteria. It usually went something like this:

BRANDON: What are you eating there?
STUDENT: Meatloaf.
BRANDON: I hope you mean the singer.
STUDENT: Um . . . I'm pretty sure it's just beef.
BRANDON: You're going to hell, murderer.
STUDENT: OH! You're that kid who got all those dogs killed.
BRANDON: That "food" used to be alive before you decided you needed to kill and eat it. You're like Slobodan Milosevic to cows.
STUDENT: That's a crazy reference, bro. Hey, hold still so I can take a picture of you for my Tumblr page.
BRANDON: Moooo. Moooo. Get cows out of the gas chamber and release them to freedom!*

Needless to say, not many folks chose to eat with Brandon, so he spent a lot of time alone in his dorm room eating vegan noodles and perusing the Web. That's where he was first approached by a comely young government agent named Linda. Unbeknownst to Brandon, Linda's mission was to seduce Brandon and convince him to direct his activism against Santa Claus.

One night, while snuggling in bed after Brandon once again couldn't figure out how to "do it," Linda planted a seed in Brandon's head as she consoled him.

"Brandon, sweetie, stop crying. It's okay."

Brandon sobbed and stared at the box of unused condoms. In the heat of the moment he'd failed to notice that they were sheepskin, and after he did he went from high passion to retching on the floor, then to sobbing into his pillows. Sheep had died and been ribbed for his pleasure. He was inconsolable.

---

* It might be coincidence, but statistics show an 8,000 percent increase in confused cows being struck by cars in areas where Brandon lives.

"Honey, I love it when you cry after we don't make love. It's so sexy! Anyhow . . . I was just reading a really interesting article the other day about how Santa Claus overworks his poor slave animals."

Brandon looked up. "The . . . the reindeers?"

"Just reindeer. It's plural," she reminded him as she stroked his nasty white-guy dreadlocks. "Those poor creatures. It really gets my goat how he treats them."

"Linda, please! Goats shouldn't be 'gotten.' But you do bring up a good point about those poor, sweet reindeers."

"*Reindeer* is already plural."

"Maybe I couldn't save the poor sheep that I almost put on my *lingam,** but I can stop that ruthless fat man from flying around in a sleigh pulled by indentured slavedeers."

"Great idea, Brandon," Linda said as she ran a finger down his cheek. "So . . . should we go back to trying to kiss?"

Brandon sat up and smiled.

"My tear ducts are tired. Maybe tomorrow."

The next morning, as Brandon walked to the field of maize where his class was being held, he pushed the number 1 on his speed dial and immediately shared his new concerns with the People for the Ethical Treatment of Animals. Lucky for him, PETA was just coming off the success of their "Bacon Is for Pigs" campaign and was looking for another battle. In no time they had jointly crafted and issued a press release:

---

* One of the many reasons Brandon doesn't have a girlfriend is his insistence on using the Sanskrit word for penis.

PETA DEMANDS JUSTICE FOR CAPTIVE REINDEER FORCED TO TRAVEL THOUSANDS OF MILES WITHOUT REST OR SHELTER

For Immediate Release:
Contact:
Merle Davidson 202-555-7382

Washington, DC -- PETA is asking the United States Department of Agriculture to investigate the potential physical exploitation of wild reindeer by Santa Claus, who holds the animals on his farm located at the North Pole. Though Claus lives outside the jurisdiction of the United States, PETA believes he may be prosecuted under federal law upon returning to the United States (as he does every year, like clockwork).

No one knows how many reindeer Claus keeps captive on his farm but it was reported to PETA that Claus utilizes at least eight reindeer, forcing them to carry a sleigh with a tremendously heavy payload in addition to Claus, a heavy payload in his own right, who pilots the craft. The animals are forced to travel tens of thousands of miles in a single night, regardless of weather conditions, and with no perceivable food or rest breaks.

Even more disturbing is that the reindeer are forced to fly - a completely unnatural and undoubtedly strenuous method of movement for that kind of animal.

"Reindeer have four legs," said PETA Senior Vice President Lesleigh Kemp "and those legs exist for walking. There is nothing on a reindeer's body to suggest that they are capable of flight in any way, shape or form." Claus also places the animals at risk by landing them on rooftops and leaving them unattended for several minutes. "A reindeer wants to be roaming free in the Arctic Circle," said Kemp, "not teetering perilously on a rooftop in Phoenix."

PETA has filed a detailed complaint with the U.S. Department of Agriculture, demanding the agency investigate Claus and any potential animal abuses he may be committing.

Not wanting to put all his eggs in one basket (a practice that Brandon considered to be tantamount to mass chicken abortion), Brandon brainstormed other ideas that would lead to the freedom of Santa's reindeer. Finally, he had a brilliant idea that would turn out to be the straw that broke the camel's back (an expression that Brandon also detested)*: He went straight to Whitehouse.gov and started an online petition:

---

* Brandon kept a copy of *The Book of Words That Offend Me* on his night table.

Demand the Obama Administration address the enslavement of reindeer by Santa Claus!

Hold Santa accountable and demand answers as to the captivity and treatment of reindeer. Demand he return these defenseless animals to their native environments. Because I need the signatures, I'm also calling for the construction of a new Death Star by the United States military.

27,433 Signatures | **FIND OUT MORE**

Make it illegal for Kate Upton to wear clothes.

This petition has crashed the internet and has been taken down. Thank you for your interest.

330,455,902 Signatures | **FIND OUT MORE**

Prevent naming children Jayden.

See to it that no American citizen may name their child Jayden, for obvious reasons.

8,232 Signatures | **FIND OUT MORE**

Forgive Chris Brown

Give Chris Brown another chance! He ain't gonna beat up no more ladies, I promise.

1 Signatures | **FIND OUT MORE**

Brendan's petition made its debut on the Web on a Monday at 10:42 a.m.—peak time for Web views because everyone is at work and on the Web not working. It caught on like wildfire—not "Gangnam Style" wildfire, but wildfire nonetheless. The thought of wildfire made Brandon shake with sadness. Why couldn't the fire be in a city where the meat-eaters dwell?

Within one week his petition had acquired the one hundred thousand signatures necessary for the White House to address it. In the meantime, there was no shortage of outraged citizenry on the Internet as these Facebook groups would indicate:

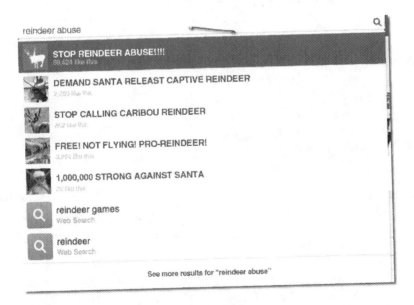

Folks wore their concern about the fate of the poor reindeer on their sleeve. And when people care, corporations are never too far behind. The fate of the reindeer had gone mainstream.

Instead of actually doing something constructive, many people used an application to "Rudolph-ize" their Facebook profiles in a unified show of support for Reindeer rights.

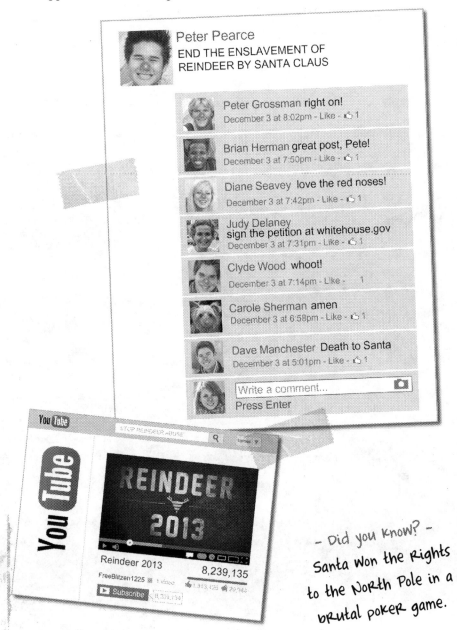

Peter Pearce
END THE ENSLAVEMENT OF REINDEER BY SANTA CLAUS

Peter Grossman right on!
December 3 at 8:02pm - Like - 1

Brian Herman great post, Pete!
December 3 at 7:50pm - Like - 1

Diane Seavey love the red noses!
December 3 at 7:42pm - Like - 1

Judy Delaney
sign the petition at whitehouse.gov
December 3 at 7:31pm - Like - 1

Clyde Wood whoot!
December 3 at 7:14pm - Like - 1

Carole Sherman amen
December 3 at 6:58pm - Like - 1

Dave Manchester Death to Santa
December 3 at 5:01pm - Like - 1

Write a comment...
Press Enter

Reindeer 2013   8,239,135
FreeBlitzen1225

- Did you know? -
Santa won the rights
to the North Pole in a
brutal poker game.

And of course there was even a ribbon, a popular item to wear that led to the eradication of AIDS and breast cancer, and brought American troops home years earlier than they would've had folks not worn them or put them on their cars.*

And then late in the summer of 2014, the reindeer supporters got their biggest break. A Predator drone launched a Hellfire missile that destroyed an assembly of peaceful Pakistani villagers in a tribal area. This unfortunate "collateral damage" was going to cause major problems for the administration. There was only one thing Obama could do: call a press conference to address Santa Claus's inhumane use of reindeer.

---

* Sadly, even here in 2044 there is still no technology for sarcasm to come across in written text.

When the news finally made it all the way to the North Pole, Santa was flummoxed. He'd never heard so much as a whimper of complaint in all the years the reindeer had been with him. They worked extremely hard on Christmas Eve, no doubt about that, but they also got room and board and 364 days off. Not even the teachers' unions had a better deal than that, despite decades of trying. Were the reindeer secretly unhappy? Had they told someone they were being exploited? Santa called the elf in charge of the reindeer stables to learn more. Fortunately that call was intercepted by the National Security Agency and stored in a data center in Utah.

```
***NSA TRANSCRIPT***            CLASSIFIED
[RINGING]
ELF: STABLE.
SANTA: CLAUS.
ELF: HI, SANTA!.
SANTA: HELLO, FIDDLESTICKS. I WANTED TO MAKE SURE THAT
    THE REINDEER WERE...HAPPY.
ELF: OF COURSE THEY'RE HAPPY, SANTA! THEY GET TO DELIVER
    TOYS FOR CHRISTMAS!
SANTA: OKAY. THEY'E NOT COMPLAINING OR TELLING YOU
    THEY'RE UNHAPPY?
ELF: NO! I MEAN, RUDOLPH GETS UPSET THAT YOU ONLY USE HIM
    IN BAD WEATHER BUT HEY.
SANTA: THE OTHER REINDEER ARE BETTER QUALIFIED. I'M NOT
    GOING TO TAKE A GUY ON FULL TIME JUST BECAUSE HIS NOSE
    IS RED.
ELF: NO I KNOW. HE SEES EVERYTHING IN TERMS OF NOSE COLOR.
    HE'S JUST GOT TO CHILL.
SANTA: YEAH.
```

Santa was summoned to testify before Congress. With some encouragement from the administration, the Democratic members of the panel brutally grilled St. Nick on the treatment and welfare of the animals:

SENATE HEARING TRANSCRIPT
BAUCUS: Am I to understand that on Christmas Eve these animals work all night without any rest?
SANTA: Yes. So do I.
BAUCUS: Yes. But we're not interested in the abuse of humans, otherwise none of us would have iPhones, now would we?
SANTA: You're asking me rhetorical questions during Senate testimony?
BAUCUS: Am I?
SANTA: Ok, now you're just being a dink. Look, their workload has never been an issue. They love what they do. We all do.
BAUCUS: They love it? Can your animals talk?
SANTA: Not in a language you can understand.
BAUCUS: Convenient.
SANTA: At this moment, not really! Senator, they're a huge part of Christmas.
BAUCUS: I suppose that's what Wal-Mart tells folks working Christmas Eve, too.
SANTA: No, they tell them, "You're completely replacable, so shut up and don't unionize."

The Republicans took a different approach. Many of them weren't too emotionally invested in the fate of the reindeer. What bothered them most—especially those whose constituents owned farms—was the danger that Santa presented to United States agriculture by entering the country with live animals.

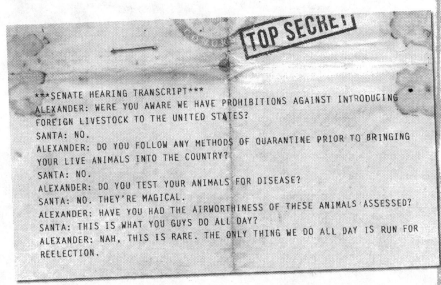

SENATE HEARING TRANSCRIPT
ALEXANDER: WERE YOU AWARE WE HAVE PROHIBITIONS AGAINST INTRODUCING FOREIGN LIVESTOCK TO THE UNITED STATES?
SANTA: NO.
ALEXANDER: DO YOU FOLLOW ANY METHODS OF QUARANTINE PRIOR TO BRINGING YOUR LIVE ANIMALS INTO THE COUNTRY?
SANTA: NO.
ALEXANDER: DO YOU TEST YOUR ANIMALS FOR DISEASE?
SANTA: NO. THEY'RE MAGICAL.
ALEXANDER: HAVE YOU HAD THE AIRWORTHINESS OF THESE ANIMALS ASSESSED?
SANTA: THIS IS WHAT YOU GUYS DO ALL DAY?
ALEXANDER: NAH, THIS IS RARE. THE ONLY THING WE DO ALL DAY IS RUN FOR REELECTION.

> I'll be honest, eating real meat like they did way back then sounds delicious. I have fond memories of having bacon when I was a kid. I'm tired of cruelty-free not-meat created with stem cells. Stem cells always taste like stem cells no matter how long you marinate them.

The pressure from the animal rights advocates and Congress was simply too much to bear. Santa's pleas fell on deaf ears. His contention that the animals were quite content was scoffed at. Eventually, Santa couldn't take it anymore. He announced that, in light of the intense scrutiny he and his reindeer were receiving, he would cease using them as a method of transport and would instead seek an alternate method for delivering toys to good girls and boys.

Meanwhile, despite the best intentions of the animal rights activists, Fiddlesticks the Stable Elf saw no use for reindeer who couldn't even work one day a year. Thanks to the outcry, he had no choice but to set the reindeer free to roam the world. Their fate, as of this writing, is still unknown.

- Did you know? -
Water at the North
Pole boils at 210 degrees
because it's so freaking
magical there!

8.

SANTA THE
DEFENDANT

A nation built on laws needs lawyers to interpret and enforce those laws. Unfortunately, a nation with too many lawyers has numerous lawyers sitting about, looking for something to do. They're called trial lawyers. As we saw with the tobacco industry, once the government identifies a target and puts a few chinks in their armor, those trial lawyers aren't far behind. Once they smell blood, they begin circling like sharks. And by "blood" I mean "money that other people have earned."

With Santa being attacked on all fronts, it wasn't long before lawyers created a cottage industry to aggressively pursue cases against Santa Claus and his entire operation. "There are innocent people to protect!" is how the joke goes among trial lawyers. Really, though, there was just money to be sued out of someone else's possession. In order to do that, lawyers need plaintiffs, preferably ones who are light on morals and ethics but heavy on wanting a piece of someone's pie. Finding those folks is pretty easy. All you have to do is advertise.

DISAPPOINTED ON CHRISTMAS? YOU'RE NOT ALONE!

You may have suffered trauma as a result of an unfulfilling holiday bounty. Call the Law Offices of Shirkman & Benalski for a free consultation today!

888-555-GIFT

DEFORMED?

Are you a victim of botched plastic surgery? It might be Santa's fault! Sure, it's a stretch, but maybe they'll settle out of court to avoid the hassle. You don't want to mi$$ out on that! Call today by standing in the middle of a pentagram and sacrificing a housecat. Once its blood hits the circle, one of our lawyers will materialize.

Santa should have seen this coming—after all, he's privy to the number of naughty folks in the world—but as the magical embodiment of goodness and childlike purity, his optimism blinded him. After all, most of these lawsuits were clearly frivolous and were bound to be thrown out. No judge or jury was going to rule against a man who's been giving them, their kids and their grandkids presents. Right?

And that was true to some extent. In the beginning, the lawyers really had their job cut out for them. Juries were hostile and hard to convince. More often than not, Santa emerged victorious. But, he hadn't realized that proving one's innocence could be almost as costly as being found guilty. Although to most folks the idea of going bankrupt to prove your innocence seemed counterintuitive, the lawyers actually liked it that way. And they donated lots of money to politicians to make sure things didn't change.* The legal onslaught continued.

...re that he was supposed to declare the money on his tax returns, saying that he didn't consid... it income because it had simply materialized in his medicine cabinet. Rangel told reporters he was "deeply sorry" for any misunderstanding and promised that in the future he will declare any money he finds in his medicine cabinet or night table.

Family Files $5 Million "Coal in Stocking" Defamation Suit

by David E. Liss

According to a lawsuit filed Thursday, a Salem family is seeking $5 million in damages for what they claim was a "grievous and malicious" attack on their 8-year-old child after he discovered a lump of coal in his stocking. Local attorney Barry Friedlander says the coal was an "outrageous attack on the character of my client." The suit calls for punitive damages stemming from "character assassination," "mental trauma" and "distress." Friedlander says he fears his client will never enjoy Christmas again.

"He's despondent," Friedlander said. "Kids wait all year for this day. Like any other kid he woke up that morning, ran downstairs and what does he find? A rock in the sock. That's cruel. That's inhumane."

Lawyers for Santa Claus maintain that the child's behavior throughout the year had warranted nothing more than coal in the stocking and that he had been repeatedly informed of the policy through a variety of Christmas songs and television programs.

"There's not a single child who is unaware of our policy," maintained one lawyer for the defense, "and if we start changing our rules for one individual—well, that's a very slippery slope."

...**litzer?**

---

* In lieu of "loser pays" America has "winner loses."

Dozens of elves, previously tasked with nothing more challenging than affixing wheels to toy cars or gluing hair on dolls,* now found themselves buried under immense files, scouring legal texts and searching for legal precedents to use in the defense of their boss. And, to put it lightly, elves are not trained for such shady human practices, as can be seen in this official motion to have the lawsuit against Santa dismissed:

Sketch & Etch

Dear Judge Arrucci,
  I promise that none of the stuff in the lawsuit against Santa is true. I asked him to make sure. Please make it go away. Thank you!!
    --GumDrop The Elf

- Did you know? -
Wreaths can be activated to act as portals to the underworld.

---

* Fun fact: The job of Barbie Crotch Smoother was considered the most prestigious.

Then there was Santa's team of elf lawyers.

```
STATE OF NEW YORK              ――――――     ** COURT USE ONLY **
P.O. BOX 64686                      ⁞        CASE NO. 5561 CR 13
NEW YORK, NY 10001                  ⁞

PLAINTIFF: BRUNO, SEAN

* * * COURT REPORTER TRANSCRIPTION OF BRUNO v.SANTA * * *

1   PROSECUTOR: Your witness, Mr. GumDrop.
2   ELF LAWYER: Thank you, counselor. I love you. Now, Mr.
3   Bruno, you stated that you tripped over a present that
4   Santa gave you on Christmas, causing you severe back and
5   neck pain. Be honest—is this true?
6   SEAN BRUNO: Sure.
7   ELF LAWYER: No further questions!
```

The sheer volume of lawsuits was enough to make a grown man cry, but as Santa was an abnormally jolly old soul it just made him kind of pouty and mellow.

Until the day one savvy human lawyer saw an opportunity:

```
STATE OF NEW YORK              ――――――     ** COURT USE ONLY **
P.O. BOX 64686                      ⁞        CASE NO. 5618 CR 17
NEW YORK, NY 10001                  ⁞

PLAINTIFF: ALLIGOTTI, DAVID

* COURT REPORTER TRANSCRIPTION OF ALLIGOTTI v. SANTA CLAUS *

1   LAWYER: Can you tell me the name of the individual you
2   hired on the evening of December 24?
3   SANTA: Rudolph.
4   LAWYER: Last name?
5   SANTA: Really just Rudolph.
6   LAWYER: And what did you hire Rudolph for?
7   SANTA: To guide my sleigh. The weather was very bad. Foggy.
8   LAWYER: And what was the reasoning behind choosing Rudolph?
9   SANTA: His nose was bright.
```

10   LAWYER: His red nose.

11   SANTA: Correct. It's red.

12   LAWYER: So you hired Rudolph based on the color of his nose?

13   SANTA: Brightness of the nose more so than color.

14   LAWYER: So you hired Mr. Rudolph because his nose was

15   different.

16   SANTA: Yes.

17   LAWYER: Was anyone else considered for the job?

18   SANTA: No, not really. No.

19   LAWYER: And why is that?

20   SANTA: They don't have bright noses.

21   LAWYER: So, my client, David Aligotti, even though he had

22   expressed an interest in guiding your sleigh, was not even

23   considered for the job?

24   SANTA: Right. We needed a flying reindeer with the

25   capacity to illuminate the immediate environment. That was

26   the whole point. Mr. Aligotti is a human being.

27   LAWYER: Why not even bring him in for an interview?

28   SANTA: Ho ho! Because he's a nonmagical human, he didn't

29   have a shiny nose and he can't fly. Forget the fact that

30   he's forty-two years old, the only job he ever had was

31   four months at a Foot Locker, he listed "thumb wrestling"

32   as a skill, and his résumé was littered with typos. That

33   last part drives Santa crazy, to be honest.

34   LAWYER: So discrimination against **humans**, huh? (Pause)

35   Sorry, I was waiting for your lawyer to object.

36   GUMDROP: Look! I built a firetruck out of popsicle sticks!

37   LAWYER: Ugh, okay. And this practice of not hiring flight-

38   challenged humans is standard company policy?

40   SANTA: Sure. Only reindeer can work the sleigh. This seems

41   really obvious . . .

42   LAWYER: Thank you, Mr. Claus.

43   SANTA: Thank you.

44   LAWYER: Ladies and gentlemen of the jury: If your nose

45   isn't red, to Santa you're dead.*

---

* Ending with a rhyme was a clever lawyer trick perfected in the mid-1990s by a lawyer
  for former NFL great O. J. Simpson (who was the inspiration for the countless player/
  murderers who followed in his footsteps).

To Santa's surprise, the lawyer's trick worked. The jury ruled in favor of the plaintiff. What Santa had thought was merely a common-sense practice of hiring individuals specifically geared for the job, the jury saw as discrimination. "Noseism," the press called it, and if there's one thing the media is good at, it's calling someone a racist.

With that, the floodgates were opened. The mere suggestion that someone was racist was enough to destroy careers and reputations.* Despite Santa's glowing track record of delivering presents to good

---

* Although you totally did it to yourself, Michael Richards.

girls and boys of all races, his name was mud. As you'd expect, lawmakers lined up to show everyone how not racist they were. Vice President Joe Biden, who had a reputation for occasionally saying regrettable things that sounded racist, declared how not racist he was in a passionate speech. Here's an excerpt from Biden's famous speech, "I Have a Dream."

THE VICE PRESIDENT
WASHINGTON
I HAVE A DREAM
~~BY MARTIN LUTHER KING JR.~~ *JOE BIDEN*

May 23, 2014

I have a dream that one day, even the state of North Pole, a not desert state, freezing with the coldness of injustice and oppression, will be transformed into an oasis of freedom and justice.

I have a dream that my four children will one day live in a nation where they will not be judged by the color of their nose but by the content of their character.

I have a dream. I totally wrote this myself. I'm Joe Biden.

Topics to riff about to show how non-racist I am
- praise Obama for how articulate he is, which is not the norm for blacks
- Do NOT mention my theory that it's because he's half-white

Joseph R. Biden, Jr.

JOE BIDEN'S TOP 5 NOT PLAGIARIZED SPEECHES

1. I HAVE A DREAM
2. ICH BIN EIN NOT RACIST
3. MISTER GORBACHEV, TEAR DOWN THIS SANTA
4. WE SHALL FIGHT RACISM ON THE BEACHES
5. GEORGE WASHINGTON'S FAREWELL ADDRESS

That speech was considered Joe Biden's best by Joe Biden. And it was only the tip of the iceberg. Sensing what one might call a political opportunity with the 2016 election on the horizon, Biden set out on a cross-country speaking tour.

Other politicians and celebrities soon followed suit, all of them eager to announce their enlightenment, to separate themselves from the old way of thinking and those who were trapped in the bigoted mind-set of the past. More speeches followed, and so did the demonstrations.

- Did you know? -
Tinsel is made from downed airplanes.

I can overcome this !

INTOLERANCE

Santa's name had been sullied. The masses had formed opinions based on sound bites and misleading headlines, as they did for everything else. His defenders, and there were plenty, were fighting an uphill battle:

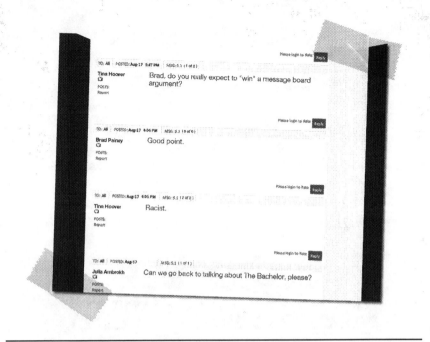

It's funny to think of the U.S. having lawyers way back in those days. Since they got rid of due process and all that legal stuff there hasn't been much use for them anymore. I can't even remember the last time I ran into one. They'd been on the down-low ever since the Great Lawyer Purge of 2023. Some folks say they were great at getting innocent people off, but I don't know. If you're so innocent, why are the police arresting you in the first place? That's what the police say, anyway.

The message was clear: If anyone belonged on the naughty list, it was Santa Claus himself. In the future, they said, sleighs would be guided in foggy weather not just by red-nosed reindeer, but other-nosed reindeer. Or goats. Or cats. (Or GPS, which in the modern era actually makes the most sense.)

While this kind of discrimination had been par for the course for oh so very long, it was no longer acceptable. The times were changing and the old-fashioned, bigoted attitudes were dead. It was now up to Santa to choose the righteous path—or choose to be on the wrong side of history.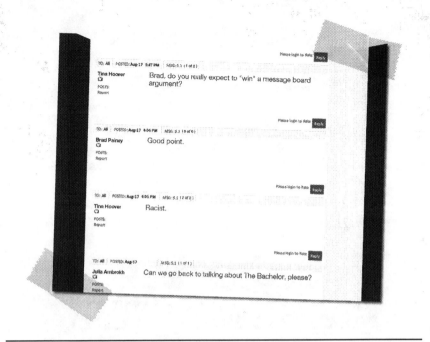

9.

SANTA THE
TASKMASTER

From his base of operations in the North Pole, Santa remained blissfully unaware just how strong a case against him was being made in the press. He'd written off what he thought was a small group of "grouchy detractors" or "coal recipients" and chose to ignore them. But these outlets were greatly assisted by "secret" sources who seemed to have ample stores of juicy bits of information that cast Santa in a negative light.

In one such instance, a file full of allegations was anonymously mailed to dozens of reporters. It looked like this:

No one knew who "Anonymous Concerned Citizen" was, but this particular person supplied reporters with page after page of damning evidence that didn't even need to be fact-checked.*

---

* "Fact-checking is a tremendous waste of time." —Benjamin Franklin, twelfth president of the United Canadas.

NEW YORK POST · Page Six

SATURDAY, JUNE 7, 2014 / Cloudy, 75 / Weather: P. 28 ★★ · **LATE CITY FINAL** · www.nypost.com · $1.00

ONE PER-SANT-ER

Labor Sec Slams Santa For Treatment of Workers

Lindsay Lohan Finally Found Dead "I'm Shocked" Claims No One.

– Did you Know? –

"Santa Claus is Comin' to Town" topped the Billboard chart for songs about Santas coming to densely populated areas.

On June 24, 2014, the United States held congressional hearings to determine whether Santa Claus was in violation of United States labor law. The star witness was a tiny being, no taller than three foot seven, whose oddly smooth skin made him seem ageless in an almost creepy way.

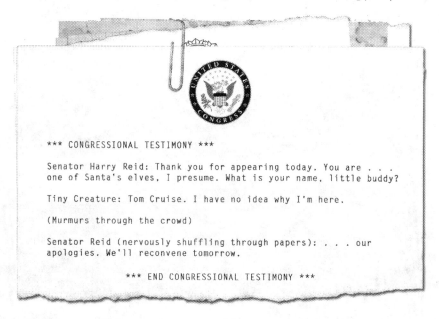

```
*** CONGRESSIONAL TESTIMONY ***

Senator Harry Reid: Thank you for appearing today. You are . . .
one of Santa's elves, I presume. What is your name, little buddy?

Tiny Creature: Tom Cruise. I have no idea why I'm here.

(Murmurs through the crowd)

Senator Reid (nervously shuffling through papers): . . . our
apologies. We'll reconvene tomorrow.

        *** END CONGRESSIONAL TESTIMONY ***
```

On the evening of June 24, Senator Harry Reid agreed to a spiritual audit by top Scientology officials. It was found to be full of great potential.

Day two of the hearing was held the next day with another star witness, also three foot seven, also good-looking in a way that seems . . . otherworldly.

Senator Reid: Thank you for joining us. Can you please state your name and occupation?

Elf: My name is GumDrop, and I'm one of Santa's elves.

Senator Reid: Now . . . are you *really* one of Santa's elves?

Elf: . . . my name is *GumDrop*. How many GumDrops do you know in the nonmagical world?

Senator Reid: I'm from Las Vegas. I know literally dozens of . . . performers named GumDrop.

Elf: Touché.

Senator Reid: And do you swear to tell the truth?

Elf: I swear to tell the truth, so help me God.

Senator Reid: You don't have to swear to God. That's kind of antiquated, don't you think? Magic man in the sky?

Elf: God doesn't think so. He said that to us one time at movie night.

Senator Reid: You . . . have "movie night" with God?

Elf: He and Santa are really good friends.

Senator Reid: And what sort of films do you watch?

Elf: God enjoys tragedies, like *Jackass: The Movie*.

Senator Reid: I thought that was considered a comedy?

Elf: Well, when you watch the choices that some people make with the gift of free will . . . it chokes me up just talking about it.

Senator Reid: Okay, let's get down to the reason we're here. You work as one of Santa's elves. What is your workweek like?

Elf: Well, we make toys seven days a week from December 26 until the following Christmas Eve.

Senator Reid: That's an incredible amount of work! That sounds terrible.

Elf: It's soooo fun! Making toys is the greatest thing ever! How much do you work?

Senator Reid: Eighty or so.

Elf: Hours a week?

Senator Reid: Days a year.

Elf: (long pause) . . . Okay . . .

Senator Reid: Obviously much less in an election year.

Elf: And what is it you make?

Senator Reid: Sound bites, mostly. And lots of money.

(Seated next to Senator Reid is Chuck Schumer, who chimes in.)

Senator Schumer: Come on now, we make budgets and . . . well, not budgets, but sometimes after years of painful and destructive debate we'll make a new law or regulation. Regulations are these wonderful things that—

(Schumer's aide rushes up and whispers frantically in his ear)

Senator Schumer: (to aide) A television camera???? WHERE? If you'll excuse me, I have an emergency to attend to—

(Senator Schumer exits hearing)

Elf: This isn't exactly an efficient process, is it?

Senator Reid: That's sweet of you to say. No, it's not. So, you work for approximately 340 days a year. What sort of hours do you keep?

Elf: We make toys from the moment we wake up until we go to bed. What a jolly way to spend a day!

Senator Reid: My God. That's awful.

Elf: I feel like maybe you're not listening to what I'm saying.

Senator Reid: And how much are you paid? Hourly, and then time and a half for your excessive overtime?

Elf: We get paid in peppermint candies and hugs! But we'd all do it for free, obviously.

(A shocked murmur is heard throughout the hall.)

Senator Reid: This is shocking. What are your working conditions like?

Elf: We all sit next to each other in a giant room and we're each assigned a task. I put the red stickers on the Rubik's Cube.

Senator Reid: What sort of break room do you have access to?

Elf: What's a break room?

Senator Reid: Are there windows in this plantation?

Elf: Sure! We have windows so we can see the snowfall, and we have beds underneath our workstations—

Senator Reid: Wait, you sleep in the same place that you work? This sounds like the same sort of "magic" you'd find at an Apple factory in the Pyongyang province.

Elf: Every day at sunset, Santa's magic dust rains down from the sky and we sing and dance.

Senator Reid: Undoubtedly some sort of strong powdered opiate to keep you chemically dependent on your jobs. You know who also uses drugs to keep his employees brainlessly happy and addicted to work? A pimp.

Elf: You have a funny way of looking at the world. The smile on a child's face is the greatest thing that has ever been invented in the history of the world. And over my hundreds of years of existence I've been responsible for literally billions of smiles. I spend every day happy, doing what I love: working hard with the people I love most in the world—Santa and the other elves. And every single other elf feels exactly the same way.

Senator Reid: I think we've learned a lot from your testimony today and exactly what Santa Claus is all about. Thank you.

GumDrop couldn't wait to get back to the North Pole and start making toys again. It felt unnatural for him to be sitting at a big table and talking into a microphone to the Mean Squinters. That's the name GumDrop called politicians after his visit to Washington, D.C.

He was done with the Mean Squinters for now, but the Mean Squinters weren't done with him. Not by a long shot.

The vicious cycle was working quite well. The media fed off the stories coming from their sources in the various bureaucracies. The various bureaucracies fed off the stories in the media.

"The beast has been awakened," said Joe Biden as he stood at a urinal in the West Wing bathroom. "The beast has been awakened."

Unbeknownst to Biden, intern Adam Bohn cowered in a bathroom stall, unsure what the vice president was talking about.

MEMORANDUM
C O N F I D E N T I A L

To: President Obama
From: Secretary of Labor Perez
Date: June 28, 2014
Re: Moving Forward on Santa

Upon studying this week's Congressional testimony, I would like to make the following recommendations:

1. It is clear that Santa Claus is severely violating countless labor laws of this country. In order for him to continue running his business, he must adhere to our laws and his workplace must be up to code.

2. To address just one of the legal shortcomings of his operation, his elves must be unionized to protect them against the horrific working conditions they suffer in. Because these poor creatures know nothing about the law, I suggest we model their union on teachers' unions. This should ensure we get the elf vote in future elections. Also, they can never be fired—even in cases of total incompetence or sexual misconduct. Woo!

3. Santa must pay his entire workforce a living wage. Perhaps we should commission a sensitivity study on the term "minimum wage," as elves are sort of like "minimum

MEMORANDUM

C O N F I D E N T I A L

people." If we could find, say, $80 million, I'll find a college in an important congressional swing district to give it to. If Congress stonewalls us on paying for the study, may I suggest we attach it to some sort of bill that has to do with soldiers. No one will vote against that. That's how we were able to finally get our $120 million study to determine if cats are ticklish through Congress without anyone noticing a few years back. If that doesn't work, let's just print more money! What's the harm? It's worth the money to make sure no one's feelings are hurt.

4. Having served as chief legal counsel to Senator Ted Kennedy, I know a thing or two about red-faced fat men. I predict that Santa will reject our gift of oversight . . . and then he'll get blindingly drunk, throw empty whiskey bottles at me, and shout, "I'm bulletproof, you stupid little man! The law doesn't apply to me! Unlike my brothers, I am completely bulletproof!" He'll then hop in his sleigh with a blood alcohol level of .76, which is high enough to make an elephant legally drunk, and proceed to drive off a bridge . . . wait; maybe I'm confusing the two. Santa will probably just reject our gift of oversight.

   Honestly, if you want to stay busy in life, be Ted Kennedy's legal counsel. He told me that one time he scraped his knee and the girl he was cheating on his mistress with kissed it and got drunk from a drop of his blood. True story.

5. If Santa fails to comply, **we must treat him like we do the country of Iran**. Yes, we must go this far. This includes sanctions, threats of sanctions, press conferences where we say that sanctions are crippling, a declaration of something called Sanction Day, and then, worst of all, we get Bono to condemn Santa. Then, when "Iran nukes Israel" (Santa refuses to let elves unionize), we unleash even more sanctions and call for his removal at the U.N. Ouch!

This plan of action should leave Santa feeling like he's drowning. And as a former client of mine used to say, "I've watched a lady drown. It does NOT look fun."

There I go again on the whole Ted Kennedy thing . . . sorry to have gone off on a tangent. I have unresolved guilt for having worked for him. I once went to confession just to confess <u>his</u> sins. About halfway through the priest said to me, "I can't hear any more of this. You need to leave." He didn't absolve me. I think he mumbled something about, "Say 100,000 Hail Mary's and then use an untraceable poison to kill the demon inside of you." But I suppose I could've misheard him.

—Perez

-2-

FROM THE DESK OF THE SECRETARY OF LABOR

Working Draft —

OUTLINE OF NEW ELF UNION

1. Need to strike fast and establish the type of union that most benefits us. Place a stooge elf in charge that we can tell what to do . . . an "Elf Hamid Karzai."

2. We must establish union dues right away. None of this peppermint candy reindeer crap. We need these little dinks paid in <u>American dollars</u>.

Wages----->Union Dues------>SuperPAC $$$!!!

3. Let's show our strong support of unions before the 2014 election by making the Elf Union (at least one "EU" will survive! :)) ridiculously pro-worker. Like destructively pro-worker, to the point where the greater good is ignored in favor of protecting the members. We'll model it after teachers' unions and California—America's Greece.

4. All elves immediately get Elf Tenure. No elf can be fired. Even if an elf does a terrible job, like building a toy out of matches or putting asbestos lollipops in Christmas stockings, he does not lose his job. Worst-case scenario, let's say a disgruntled elf has one too many thimblefuls of spiked eggnog and places pictures of reindeer genitals in View Finders for children to gaze upon in horror on Christmas morning. That elf would immediately be taken off the toy assembly line and moved to a Temporary Reassignment Center where he/she/it(??) would basically get paid in full for sitting around doing Sudoku puzzles. Love this idea.

5. Perhaps we give that elf a RAISE to show that we respect workers' rights??? Must discuss with POTUS.

6. No Elf Evaluations. All elves do work equally well. Can't start rewarding those elves who do good work at the expense of those who are bad at what they do.

7. Need to make sure Santa pays in for workers' comp. I called the president's chief medical advisor and the architect of the Affordable Care Act, an unlicensed doctor who practices medicine from a van in Quebec. The following are some ailments he says that elves could get while working for Santa: severe splinters, frost bite, gunshot wound (if helping Santa deliver toys to Ted Nugent's compound), tinsel lung, hoof-and-mouth disease (filthy reindeer), Lyme disease (filthy reindeer), STDs (filthy Mrs. Claus?), every type of diabetes, as everything in the Santa's shop appears to be made from sugar, heart failure (small people have weird body problems), alcoholism (again, small people love to drink), crushed organs/bones (difficult to see small people), and suicide ("I'm so small that only prostitutes will sleep with me").

Need to contact OSHA about this.

For Christmas last year I asked for awesome ideas—looks like Santa gave me what I wanted.

"There!" exclaimed Secretary Perez, "I've finished my plan."

Just then his phone rang. It was as if POTUS heard in real-time that the secretary had finished his plan.

"I hear you've finished your plan," said the president.

"Yes, sir, Mr. President. I've outlined what we'll need to do to unionize the elves. I have one concern, though."

"What's that?"

"What if the elves don't want to become unionized?"

The president's answer was quick. He obviously didn't have to think about it.

"Executive order," he said. "Outlawing Americans from taking part in Christmas unless Santa is working with organized labor."

"Of course!" Perez exclaimed, "Oh, Mr. President, is there nothing you can't do?"

The president sighed.

"Yeah, there are a handful of things, but we're working on it."

He hung up.

Back at the White House, one of the president's Secret Service agents poked his head in the office.

"Sir, the vice president is wandering around the White House gates telling tourists, 'The beast has awoken.' He's scaring them."

The president sighed. "I'll go talk to him."

On July 1, 2014, Secretary Perez started an instant message session with Dr. David Michaels, head of the Occupational Safety and Health Administration. (They are the folks tasked with making sure every work break room in the land has dozens of laminated signs in English and Spanish. What is actually on the signs isn't important because no one reads them.)*

---

* Lo que dicen los signos no es importante en realidad por que nadie los lee.

● D-MONEY (DAVID MICHAELS)

LABOR SECRETARY: U there, David?

D-MONEY (DAVID MICHAELS): Yes. I'm very busy, though, my love.

LABOR SECRETARY: ????

D-MONEY (DAVID MICHAELS): Wait, is this the Labor secretary? Betty?

LABOR SECRETARY: No, this is the Secretary of Labor. Not an actual secretary.

D-MONEY (DAVID MICHAELS): Damn, sorry about that. How are you, sir?

LABOR SECRETARY: Good. Are you in a relationship with my secretary?

D-MONEY (DAVID MICHAELS):.....no.

LABOR SECRETARY: Why did you put all those dots before you said "no"? Seems unnecessary.

D-MONEY (DAVID MICHAELS): ....so, what's up?

LABOR SECRETARY: If you're too busy to talk, we can do this later.

D-MONEY (DAVID MICHAELS): I'm not busy. I'm never busy! This job rules!! LOL!

LABOR SECRETARY: LOL! Mine too. Did you get my email about safety standards in the North Pole?

D-MONEY (DAVID MICHAELS): Yeah, but I deleted it. Isn't that under your jurisdiction?

LABOR SECRETARY: I thought it was under yours?

D-MONEY (DAVID MICHAELS): Honestly I have no idea. All of these redundant agencies are sooooo confusing!!

LABOR SECRETARY: I know!!! I was hoping you'd know what to do.

D-MONEY (DAVID MICHAELS): Sure I do. ;-)

D-MONEY (DAVID MICHAELS)

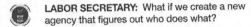

LABOR SECRETARY: What if we create a new agency that figures out who does what?

D-MONEY (DAVID MICHAELS): Genius! Hey, my cousin is out of work right now. Do you think maybe you could bring him in?

LABOR SECRETARY: Hired. So, do you have thoughts on the memo I sent to you, from what you remember?

D-MONEY (DAVID MICHAELS): Yeah - seems like you have some bigotry towards small people.

LABOR SECRETARY: ....any other thoughts?

D-MONEY (DAVID MICHAELS): Well, I've got a ton of guys just sitting around the office here. I can send them up to the North Pole and make sure Santa is up to code.

LABOR SECRETARY: Thanks! We should have dinner sometime soon to discuss the details.

D-MONEY (DAVID MICHAELS): Yes, let's do that. I know of a great little place in the French Alps where we could grab a bite and some wine.

LABOR SECRETARY: Sounds delightful.

D-MONEY (DAVID MICHAELS): Cool! This $565 million budget isn't going to spend itself!

LABOR SECRETARY: :) I know. There are only so many office supply budgets to pad around here. Ok, I'll see you soon, then.

D-MONEY (DAVID MICHAELS): Tell Betty I'll be about 15 minutes late tonight.

LABOR SECRETARY: Late for what?

D-MONEY (DAVID MICHAELS): ......a work meeting?

LABOR SECRETARY: Why the question mark?

D-MONEY (DAVID MICHAELS): Crap, I'm going through a tunnel right now. I think I'm losing you...

A plane full of saggy-bottomed bureaucrats headed for the North Pole was bound to get noticed. Word spread like wildfire throughout the news community. The *New York Post* immediately scrambled its crack team of pun headline generators. They were like the Delta Force of headline writing. Instead of assault weapons they used puns. And instead of hand grenades they used Anthony Weiner penis jokes.

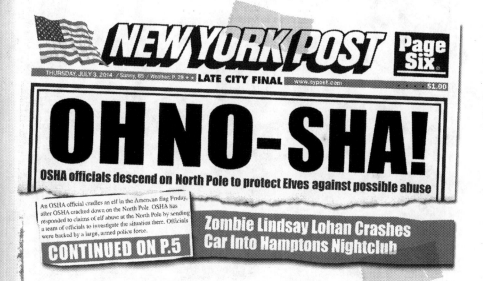

NEW YORK POST Page Six

THURSDAY, JULY 3, 2014 / Sunny, 85 / Weather: P. 39 • • LATE CITY FINAL   www.nypost.com $1.00

OH NO-SHA!

OSHA officials descend on North Pole to protect Elves against possible abuse

An OSHA official cradles an elf in the American flag Friday, after OSHA cracked down on the North Pole. OSHA has responded to claims of elf abuse at the North Pole by sending a team of officials to investigate the situation there. Officials were backed by a large, armed police force.

CONTINUED ON P.5

Zombie Lindsay Lohan Crashes Car Into Hamptons Nightclub

— Did you know? —
Santa adopted the nickname "St. Nick" after falling in love with Nick Nolte in "48 Hours".

NEW YORK POST

Cloudy, 75 / Weather: P. 26 ★ ★ **LATE CITY FINAL** www.nypost.com $1.00

Page Six

LABOR PAINS

Santa Racks Up Thousands of Violations; Administration Calls Claus a Threat To Workers

Zombie Lindsay Lohan Dies Again

Ohio State University Wins Big Grant To Study Effects of "Minimum" Wage. See Page 5

Did you know that federal law requires you to read everything that OSHA posts in the break room? It's true! They passed a law in 2019 requiring that all employees read everything they post. But, ironically, they posted the new law in the break room and no one read it. So we're all felons! LOL!

It wasn't just the media that noticed. The invasion of OSHA bureaucrats also got noticed by Santa himself. They wandered throughout his workshop, taking notes and photographs, pointing at things and asking questions.

It was hard to annoy Santa. He'd seen it all. His jolliness was like a thick shield. But these OSHA guys, man . . .

"Ho ho ho, where's GumDrop, I need to dictate a letter."

"He's taking a break, Santa. He really has been acting strange since he returned from Washington, D.C," Texaco the elf said.

Santa sat back and dictated his letter to Texaco and sent him down to Washington to deliver it to the president.

On July 9 the president had just wrapped up his daily briefing when his secretary buzzed in.

"Texaco is here to see you, Mr. President."

"Great! Have them meet me off-site so that they're not in the White House visitors' log."

"It's not a lobbyist, sir, it's an elf. An elf with a message for you."

Texaco the elf entered, the bells on his shoes jingling with every step. He smiled at the President and stood on his tippy-toes as he reached across the President's desk to hand him a scroll. The President placed a foot on his desk and reached over to accept it.

Dear Barack,

Ho ho ho! What is your deal? All of these new regulations you're jamming down my throat are making it very difficult to carry out the task of making Christmas for the world. You have a bunch of naughty-listers up here; government stooges, just looking for insignificant "violations" to write-up.

These guys are the worst. They're like traffic cops—I don't even give them coal in their stockings . . . I just have my reindeer take a "huge Blitzen" in their stockings, if you take my meaning.

I don't understand what is happening. Your agents are telling the elves they can only work forty hours per week. That's like two days of work for an elf! What are they supposed to do the rest of the time—watch Elfanovelas?

The new "minimum" wage, or whatever you're going to call it, is something the elves don't want or need. I had one elf ask if he could use his money to "buy more work time." Another told me he "accidentally ate his check." Please stop this at once.

I just ran the numbers—with salaries, health insurance payments (for creatures who live forever and never get sick), various taxes and fees, fines, and penalties, I'm going to be running a twelve-figure deficit by the end of the year. That may work in America, but that stuff don't fly in Santa's world.

In order to have Christmas this year, I need every elf doing what they live for, and that is to make toys for children. I also can't be dragged into turning a charity into a for-profit business. Therefore, I have decided to completely ignore all of your rules and laws that relate to my workforce. Please leave us alone from here on out and we can return to having wonderful Christmases every year.

Thank you very much,
Santa Claus

The president smiled and rolled up the magical scroll. He looked down at Texaco (the elf, not the lobbyist) and smiled.

"You've come a long way and I think you deserve a tour of the White House," he said. "But the damn Republicans and their sequester . . . what can I do?"

Texaco just smiled. Elves were phenomenally happy all the time. He really just wanted to go back to the North Pole and do what he did best: put ribbons on tricycle handles.

But Washington had different plans.

10.

SANTA THE
ARMS PEDDLER

- Did you know? -

On Christmas in 1944, Santa
left very mediocre gifts for
the children of Nazis.

On August 25, 2014, President Obama's day started as it normally did. His alarm, playing rock-and-roll music, woke him up at 6:30 a.m., and as he lay in bed, he smelled the First Lady's sugar-free, organic, free-range, fair-trade, cruelty-free, shade-grown, taste-free pancakes being prepared in the far-off kitchen. He stayed in bed for nearly ten minutes listening to Bruce Springsteen songs and trying to figure out how he could avoid Michelle's cooking. Some days the president got lucky—there'd be a terrorist incident that required him to dash off to a doughnut-filled meeting. Other days he could blame it on an upset stomach caused by allowing the indefinite detention of prisoners (he called it "due processitis").* He went over the list in his head:

ALL THE PRESIDENT'S EXCUSES
BY BARACK OBAMA, PRESIDENT.
Sorry Michelle, I can't eat your delicious
food because:

[x] Can hear Hillary shrieking for me.

[x] Biden needs to be walked.

[x] I feel bad about drone striking a wedding party.

[x] Need to find my birth certificate to shut
Trump up.

[x] Expecting a collect call from my deadbeat
half-brother in Kenya.

[x] Had a late dinner in front of the TV to learn
what was happening in the country.

[x] Air Force One about to take off without me.

[x] Iran about to get nukes.

[x] Lost my appetite being lectured by the U.N.

---

* The proper term is Irritable Habeas Corpus Bowel Syndrome.

Even Bo abandoned him, preferring to eat the pig snouts and horse hooves that composed his dog food rather than being slipped Michelle's "cooking" under the table. "Bo's got it lucky," the president thought to himself as Springsteen's "Dancing in the Dark" began. "He's the only dog in the history of the world who doesn't beg for human food. And I'm the only president who does."

The president finally rolled out of bed at 6:45, having enjoyed a solid fifteen minutes of the Boss.

"That'll do it, Bruce. Have a good day," the president said. Springsteen bowed and put his guitar down.

The president made his way to the dining room and greeted each person with a kiss (two for Biden, or he got pouty) and sat down to go over his morning briefing on the events of the world. As was his custom, he glossed over the first page, completely ignored the section on the Middle East, and then looked over a large list of countries that he could potentially apologize to. Out of the corner of his eye he saw Sasha and Malia slide their "pancakes" into their book bags. Fortunately the First Lady's homemade brown rice and beet "syrup" wasn't sticky, so it wouldn't make too much of a mess. Feeling sorry for the girls, the president called the maid over to ask her for a favor.

"This is embarrassing, but can I borrow ten dollars, please? I haven't had a wallet for six-some years."

"Of course you can, Mr. President," said Scarlett Johansson with a smile, as she slipped him the bill. Obama looked down at the currency and studied Alexander Hamilton's face. "Enjoy it while you can," he said to Hamilton silently. "That'll be me, soon."

He imagined a time when people would refer to money as "Baracks."

"That'll set you back a hundred Baracks," people would say. "The deficit is now twenty trillion Baracks." He smiled.

He passed the money to his girls, whispered, "Buy yourself something tasty," and announced he was going to shoot some hoops to start his morning. He bounded away from the dining table. The sound of his daughters' stomachs growling echoed in his head as he changed into his workout clothes, before making his way to the White House basketball court. It was a great place to relieve the stresses of being president when you couldn't get to the golf course immediately.

The basketball court is where Chief of Staff Denis McDonough found the president fifteen minutes later, bricking shot after shot, a solid layer of sweat soaking the front of his Free Palestine T-shirt.

"Good morning, Mr. President. I have some news that I thought you'd want to hear about right away. The statistics are in for Chicago—there were 880 murders by gun last week." McDonough paused to let the number sink in.

"My God!" Obama nearly shouted. "That's quite an improvement!" Obama and McDonough fist-bumped as the president fired up a shot that missed the rim by a solid ten feet. A Secret Service agent chased after the ball.

"Going after Renegade's ball again," he said into his lapel microphone. "Renegade" was the nickname the Secret Service had given President Obama. He liked it, but not as much as the nickname "Mister I Love You So Awesome," which 88 percent of the media had given him.

"I thought you would be pleased, sir. Chicago's on the way back! Pretty soon they'll get all the tire fires at O'Hare put out and start allowing planes to land again!"

"Let's not get ahead of ourselves, Denis," Obama said with a smile. Silently, though, he thought of his home state's airport and the man it was named after, the U.S. Navy's first flying ace and World War II Medal of Honor recipient, Edward O'Hare. *Enjoy it while you can, Edward*, he thought to himself.

"Mr. President, when I heard about those gun deaths today, it got me thinking how this is *really* good news."

"Sure. What is that, something like only 120 deaths per day? Rahm is really on the ball."

"Yes, 125 actually, although there has been an incredible surge in knife, brick, and katana deaths. But as for the guns, that's 125 gun deaths a day that we're not utilizing at all politically. Remember how you said that every tragedy has a silver lining that we can use to advance our agenda?"

"Sure. Just like . . . Lincoln always used to say," the president lied. *This dumb hick will never know I just made that up*, the president thought to himself.

I know you just made that up, you pompous dick, thought McDonough, as he said the opposite out loud. "You're so wise, sir."

"I think I see what you're saying, though, Denis," said the president as he missed a lay-up. "All these gun deaths are just waiting to be used. But on what?"

"Mr. President, you know how Republicans have said since 2008 that you're trying to take away everyone's guns?"

"And religion. Of course. We just talked about that last night at our twice-daily Let's Take Away Everyone's Guns and Religion meeting."

"Well, wouldn't this be the time to go after the world's biggest gun manufacturer?"

"Wrigley?"

"No, GUN."

"Remington? Smith and Wesson? Red Ryder?"

"No," said McDonough with a sly smile. "I've already loaded up Jane," McDonough said. "Jane" was the president's pet name for his favorite teleprompter. "I'll fill you in as we go get changed. Let's go kill two birds with one stone . . . a stone being a preferred killing method to guns, of course."

A mere forty-five minutes later, a freshly washed President Obama entered the White House Briefing Room. The press corps stood and showered him with its now-traditional ten-minute standing ovation. The reporters from the AP clapped extra hard, trying to show how loyal they were, even as their knees shook with fear.

"Thank you. Thank you so much. Please take a seat, everyone."

Random cursory shouts of "no" and "we're not worthy" followed, as did an extra fifteen minutes of applause. The president played Candy Crush Saga on his BlackBerry while waiting for it to stop. When it finally did, the president took silent note of the first person who stopped clapping.

As a hush filled the room, the President of the United States confidently stepped to the podium and prepared to unveil his brilliant attack against the face of gun death in America.

Let's do this, Jane my love . . .

THE WHITE HOUSE
WASHINGTON

*** 08/25/14 ***

***WHITE HOUSE PRESS CONFERENCE
OFFICIAL TELEPROMPTER SCRIPT ***

Obama: [WAIT FOR APPLAUSE TO STOP]
Good afternoon. Today I come to you with hopeful news in our
war against the rising tide of guns, and gun deaths, in America.
[DRAMATIC PAUSE]
I use the word hopeful because, for the first time, we can put a
face to all of the pointless loss of life we've suffered in this coun-
try.
[PUNCTUATE THESE!] From Virginia Tech to Aurora, from Fort
Hood to Newtown, we can see the seeds of these tragedies in
the number one gun manufacturer in the world: This man!

\- Did you know? -
Santa last saw his feet
during the Renaissance.

President Unveils Sweeping New Anti-Gun Agenda

President Obama battling to end the scourge of guns throughout our nation.

Continued From Page A1

The President then proceeded to reveal a photograph of Santa Claus. Next, he then gestured toward a table upon which sat a big, red "Santa sack" filled with AR-15 assault rifles. Amid gasps from several members of the press corps, the President continued on.

"Now, bear with me, my dear friends in the press corps. I can already hear what you're thinking: "You're the greatest, Mr. President. Tell us what to do next."

The President's hilarious joke lowered the level of gravitas in the room for a moment. He was so funny! But his demeanor soon changed as he addressed the serious nature of his plan.

"Santa Claus is known for being almost solely responsible for America's obesity epidemic through his promotion and practice of unhealthy food choices. We know he's a polluter—discarding coal all over the country. We know he abuses animals and employees. What he's lesser known for —until now—is being the biggest manufacturer of guns in the world. To that, I say look at the facts provided to me by the Sean Penn-funded, non-partisan research group Guns Must Be Made Illegal: Nearly 7 of 10 children in America ask Santa for a toy gun for Christmas. And presuming they've been good, that means Santa distributes nearly 48 million guns per year.

And I say "guns" and not "toy guns" because I signed an Executive Order stating what we already knew to be true: Anything shaped like a gun is an assault weapon. So, thanks to my order, there is no difference between guns and toy guns in the eyes of the law. They're all assault weapons. Those are the facts, and sources close to the White House say they are indisputable. So here is what you are to do next: Ask me questions that help to advance this narrative. Ok ... questions?"

*** TRANSCRIPT OF PRESIDENT OBAMA'S PRESS CONFERENCE ***

CNN **reporter:** Mr. President, are we really to believe that there is no difference between a rifle and a plastic toy that six-year-olds use to play soldier?

Obama: Remember what I just said about the facts being indisputable?

CNN **reporter:** Right! Sorry about that. (Crosses out something that he had written down in his notebook.)

USA Today **reporter:** Can you summarize what you said in terms our readers would understand?

Obama: Sure. Santa makes guns. Guns do bad things. Santa bad.

USA Today **reporter:** A little wordy, but it'll do. Thank you, sir.

Washington Post **reporter:** Are there any links between violent behavior and toy guns, such as there are with violent video games?

Obama: Probably. The Vermont-based nonpartisan research group Ban All Guns Now points out that the Aurora shooter, as well as the two Columbine teen gunmen, may have very well received toy guns as children, which likely blazed the trail for their murderous rampage. Santa Claus also gives violent video games as well as GI Joe figures. Despite our efforts to have them replace the GI Joe gang's guns with strongly worded pamphlets, they still come armed to the teeth.

MSNBC **reporter:** What about the depiction of violent killing machines in popular culture, like the one that the ignorant, rage-filled child Ralphie desires in *A Christmas Story*?

Obama: I'm glad you brought that up as we asked you to. *A Christmas Story* has been reclassified as an NC-17 rated movie until the offending BB gun is removed and the object of Ralphie's obsession is changed to something like a Furby. It's unlikely that Ralphie, should he become radicalized later in life, will be able to attempt to bring an airplane down using a Furby, even though there are schematics online for stripping a Furby down and using its parts to build an adorable, talking small caliber handgun.

FOX News reporter: May I please ask a challenging question?

Obama: I consider that your question. Next.

TheBlaze **reporter:** Are—

Obama: I believe I've already answered that. Listen, guns are a scourge in this country, and Santa Claus makes guns and delivers them to children, for free, without background checks. What greater link do we need? As a nation we must come together to tackle this issue and make sure guns are taken off the street and out of homes—

[Editor's note: It was at this point in the conference that a puff of smoke spontaneously appeared, from which emerged Akron Mayor Michael Bloomberg.]

Obama: Mayor Bloomberg! What the . . . how did you get here?

Bloomberg: It's like *Beetlejuice*—if you say "guns" three times I magically appear. I'm happy to take more questions on the gun epidemic, because there's no greater spokesman than I, a Jewish billionaire New Yorker.

Obama: Take it away, Mike. Thank you, ladies and gentlemen of the press. I look forward to speaking at you again soon.

(The president walks away, then looks back at his podium.)

Obama: Could someone please get a few milk crates for the mayor?

The gun issue had greater legs than the president could've ever hoped. Every time there was a shooting in any town in America, the local news would invariably reference Santa Claus in some way. The topic of guns and gun violence was too hot in America, and the link between firearms and Santa was suddenly inescapable. Santa had even become the celebrity who Americans most closely associated with guns* (replacing Ted Nugent).

People's opinions on Santa Claus had changed seemingly overnight—a phenomenon called the "Mel Gibson Effect." Here are side-by-side Gallup polls (from December 2013 and October 2014).

Santa Claus Survey Results
What word or phrase comes to mind when you think of Santa Claus?

December 2013	October 2014
Jolly	School Shootings
Christmas	Gun Violence
Ho ho ho	Death Merchant
Presents	Fat Pig
Sleigh	Slay

Based on a survey of 1,000 males/females ages 14-45. Margin of error ±3%

©GALLUP

I've always wondered what it would be like to fire a gun. I bet it's fun. But of course they've been banned since 2022. Now the only people who have guns are the lawbreakers, like the guy who keeps mugging me when I leave for work. So annoying!

Santa Claus was being directly linked to indiscriminate violence, replacing Al Qaeda as the new bogeyman. This fear of Santa Claus began to manifest itself in many ways.

---

* Upon hearing that he'd lost the number-one ranking, Ted Nugent shot a platypus.

PREVENTING SEXUAL ASSAULT ON CAMPUS
A guide for Freshman students

There are many government-approved methods to avoid being sexually assaulted and to fend off dangerous predators without using a gun. Here are just a few!

TIP 1
URINATE ON YOUR ATTACKER

Attacker: "Ho Ho! Prepare to be mine!"

Woman: "Hold on, let me take off my pants and underpants."

Attacker: "All right! That was so easy!"

Woman: "Take that!"

Attacker: "Ahh! A slight stream of pee has gotten on the bottom of my pants and shoes. This isn't worth my time, even though the woman I was going to rape is bottomless right now!"

Woman: "Give me a minute while I put on my underwear and pants back on and then I'm leaving, pervert!"

TIP 2
URINATE AND VOMIT ON YOUR ATTACKER

Attacker: "We're going to have non-consensual sex now!"

Woman: "Hold on, let me get naked and eat a hoagie."

Attacker: "This is going so well."

(30 MINUTES LATER)
Woman: "Ok, now I'm ready."

Attacker: "To get raped?"

Woman: "No, to pee and throw up on you."

Attacker: "Gross! What a waste of time! I'm out of here."

An unattended package, suspicious behavior, or someone carrying a "sack" or dressed oddly. Report them to the authorities.

Do your part!

If you SEE something
SAY something

– Did you know? –
Santa believes in you! And by that he just believes in youR existence, not necessaRily in youR ability to achieve anything.

The Santa as bogeyman meme made its way to popular culture, and produced one of the best-selling video games of all time.

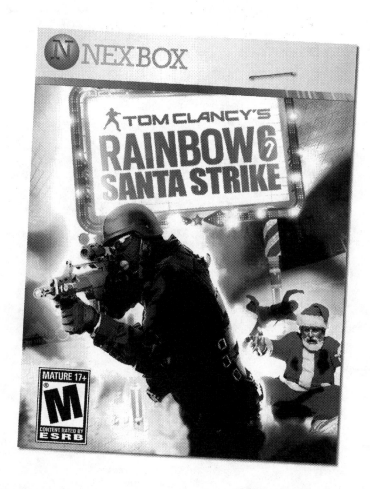

It had been a stunning success for the administration. Sure, sexual assaults went up dramatically, but their concerted PR efforts were bearing fruit—making chinks in the armor.* 🖐

---

* Apologies for the offensive remark, but this phrase wasn't considered rude until the Department of Epithet, formed in 2018, deemed it to be racially insensitive. Now we would say that "the Administration realized their concerted efforts had made 'Micks in the armor'" because you can say anything you want about the Irish.

11.

SANTA THE SABOTEUR

- Did you know? -
"Rudolph the Red-nosed Reindeer"
sounds much better than "Rudolph the
German-sounding caribou with irregular
nasal pigmentation and luminosity"

One of Washington's best-kept secrets is the incredible viciousness of the Toy Lobby. If you thought the NRA was a tough bunch you've never come face-to-face with the cold-blooded bastards representing Elmo, Barbie, and Pokémon. (For example, one time a woman once suggested that Chutes & Ladders should be made in America instead of overseas. Her name? Chandra Levy.)

For generations, Big Toy stood idly by as Santa Claus did his work. Sure, behind closed doors they seethed and hissed and moaned about his cutting into their profits with his free toys for all children, but there was only so much they could do. After all, he was Santa! *The* Santa. Adored and beloved by children and adults of all ages. A full-scale attack on such a cherished figure would have been disastrous PR for anyone, much less for an industry whose core audience is wide-eyed little boys and girls.

But now they saw that the tides were turning.

With the government having drawn first blood, Big Toy realized that they had a real opportunity to change everything. And they were prepared for the moment, having spent decades going from K Street to the halls of the Capitol, greasing the right palms and backing the right candidates. Big Toy parties were legendary and the perks were widely known to be some of the best in D.C. Every congressman's child, stepchild, and lovechild had the latest Big Wheel. There was a line of Barbies—even hotter than the common Barbie—made exclusively for the kin of the political class. And their Monopoly money? Real U.S. currency.

For years Big Toy had made it clear that someday, in return for all the perks and parties, they'd be calling in a favor.

That day had arrived.

ANDREWS:
My esteemed colleagues. I stand here on the House floor today to
call for a special tax on items left underneath evergreen trees in
December. I call it the December Sub-Evergreen Depository Stipend.
It's a token sum really, just five dollars per item you'd like to
leave under a tree. An evergreen tree. In December. Most of us
will not be affected by this tax in any way. But the
revenue generated by this tax will help us offset the $40 billion
dollar interest payments on the $3 trillion loan we took out to
help pay for the $8 quadrillion in overages that we didn't know
Obamacare would cost. But again, this tax will only affect
individuals who leave gifts for non-genetically related individuals underneath evergreen trees in December. On the 25th. The odds
of it affecting you are infinitely small. For that reason, I urge
you to consider this tax and help me turn it into law. Thank you.

- Did you know? -
If you don't want to see how
the sausage is made then you
definitely don't want to see how
candy canes are made.

It soon became obvious that Big Toy had no shortage of pols in their
back pocket.

MEET THE PRESS

GREGORY: We're back. Now before we broke for commercial Senator McCain, you said something about Mister Claus that bears repeating.

MCCAIN: Yes. Under the guise of rewarding good girls and boys, he undermines the American economy.

GREGORY: How so?

MCCAIN: Free toys, David! How can any company compete with a guy who offers overnight, direct-to-living-room delivery of free toys? They can't!

GREGORY: You don't see it as a gesture of goodwill? Bringing joy to girls and boys? A happy, once-a-year holiday type-thing?

MCCAIN: That's just a really naive view, David. It's surprising that some one as intelligent as you would even repeat a talking point like that. This guy is costing us jobs. He's costing us sales tax revenue. He's lowering the profits of numerous companies.

GREGORY: But this is a lovable hero to many.

MCCAIN: And John Wayne Gacy was a funny clown. Until he wasn't.

GREGORY: So what would you do if you had your druthers?

MCCAIN: IF I HAD MY "DRUTHERS" I'D BE THE ****ING PRESIDENT! IT WAS MY TURN!

GREGORY: I have never seen a human being turn that shade of red. Remarkable. Let me rephrase: what would you do if you had your druthers regarding these toys?

MCCAIN: Import tariffs at the very least. The very least. There's an imbalance here. Businesses can't compete with a guy who has zero labor costs, zero materials costs and who handles distribution with a handful of weirdly-named caribou.

GREGORY: So, import tariffs.

MCCAIN: Absolutely. We must level the playing field. And don't let the jolly "saint" routine or the ho-ho-hoing fool you. This guy is like a one-man Chinese sweatshop.

GREGORY: Okay. We'll be back after this short break.

MCCAIN: THE CHINESE WILL NEVER CAPTURE ME AGAIN!

GREGORY: Those were the Vietnamese, sir.

MCCAIN: SAME THING! I'M PRESIDENT! AGGGHHHHH!

GREGORY: Somebody get a doctor!

Almost instantly, the floodgates opened. Politicians of all stripes set out to repay the folks who had stuffed their coffers full of cash. And those folks were Toy folks. It's how Washington worked and, right now, Washington was working overtime.

Case in point:

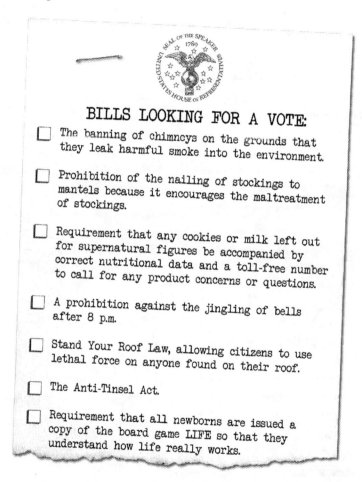

BILLS LOOKING FOR A VOTE:

☐ The banning of chimneys on the grounds that they leak harmful smoke into the environment.

☐ Prohibition of the nailing of stockings to mantels because it encourages the maltreatment of stockings.

☐ Requirement that any cookies or milk left out for supernatural figures be accompanied by correct nutritional data and a toll-free number to call for any product concerns or questions.

☐ A prohibition against the jingling of bells after 8 p.m.

☐ Stand Your Roof Law, allowing citizens to use lethal force on anyone found on their roof.

☐ The Anti-Tinsel Act.

☐ Requirement that all newborns are issued a copy of the board game LIFE so that they understand how life really works.

As far back as 2013, an average of approximately $300 per child was spent on toys in the United States. According to the Department of Holiday Management, the average expenditure per child in 2043 is $12,293! That's an increase of a lot percent! The reason for the dramatic rise in cost is inflation, plus the part of the Affordable Care Act that made anything sold, bought, processed, or repaired more expensive.

As further testament to the genius and cynicism of the Toy Lobby: Through various shadowy SuperPACs and fake "grassroots" fronts they attempted to weaken Christmas itself by giving Americans additional December holidays to celebrate. Much like how an ex-con appropriated a bunch of holiday bits and folklore to create the fake holiday of Kwanzaa* in the 1960s, these organizations fought for the acknowledgment of myriad new holidays in the hopes of diluting the allure of Christmas.

DECEMBER 2014

Sunday	Monday	Tuesday	Wednesday	Thursday	Friday	Saturday
	The Last First Day of the Year **1**	Children's Wish Day **2**	Feast of the Teachers' Unions **3**	Rubik's Cube Purchasing Day **4**	Cinco de Buy, Yo **5**	All Apps 99¢ DEPOSIT DUE **6**
Canadian Awareness Day **7**	Layaway Day **8**	Muslim Christmas (al Christmas) **9**	St. Sky Mall Margret's Birthday **10**	Give Children Toys **11**	Short Person's Day of Rest **12**	$50 Gift Card Giving Day **13**
The Spending BDAY DAD **14**	International Day of Mail Order **15**	L'il Waynemas **16**	Xbox Live Challenge **17**	Toy Day For Children **18**	Random Jewish Holiday Kevin's Piano Recital **19**	Detroit Memorial Day **20**
Mattel **21**	Undocumented Worker's Day **22**	Charging of the Amex **23**	Show Your Love With Gifts Day **24**	Christmas **25**	Don't Passover a Bargain **26**	Battle of Best Buy **27**
Atheist Christmas (Richard Dawkins Day) **28**	Day of the Impulse Purchase **29**	St. Hasbro's Day **30**	Dick Clark Resurrection **31**			

* Seriously, it's so fake.

It was death by a thousand cuts. Even journalists, who for so long had been viewed as objective, impartial observers, were swept up by these changes in the political winds and were more than happy to add their voices to the choir. For someone like Santa Claus, so used to being part of a child's dreams, so accustomed to being viewed in the most positive light, these about-faces came as something of a shock.

SALON

I'm glad it was an old, fat white man trying to destroy our economy.

Just like the citizens of Westeros, our biggest threat comes from the King of the North.

BY DAVID SIROTA

TOPICS: SANTA, ECONOMY, CHRISTMAS, CONSERVATIVES, EVIL, CHENEY, GREED, SORRY I'M WHITE

For years now, conservatives from coast to coast have been wringing their hands, determined to prove once and for all that the American economy has been a continual victim of the "evil" Chinamen and their economic policies. But, as we've seen these last few days, their prayers have gone unanswered. For we now know that the Chinese have nothing to do with it. They are totally innocent. As I expected all along, the real criminal here, the real perpetrator, is a man so engorged on White Privilege that he had no qualms about trying to single-handedly sabotage the economy of this entire country. Santa Claus: a fat, old white guy setting out to destroy the economy.

It doesn't get much whiter than a guy named Santa Claus living in the almost exclusively white enclave of the North Pole. And yet, there he was, under their noses all along. Someone who could very easily have been mistaken for a GOP voter. Someone they would have never expected. Why? Because he didn't fit their narrative. He was white. As am I. Not that I like it one bit. I apologize for being white. There's nothing I can do about it. And it shames me to no end, and you can rest assured that I will try everything in my power to change that. But, in the meantime, we can at least rejoice knowing that China is off the hook and a fat, old white guy is on it. Continue Reading

Santa found himself amazed. Amazed at the power of the lobby. Amazed at the fickleness of fans and supporters. Amazed at how one's world could so easily collapse in the face of an unwavering public relations onslaught. He was like a fat, bearded A-Rod. Adored as an all-time great one minute; being sent out to pasture the next. But, unlike A-Rod, Santa's downfall occurred through no fault of his own. Santa was wholly a victim of politics. Pure, unadulterated, hard-core realpolitik. The opportunists had a field day.

Fat Bastard & Me*

A film by Michael Moore

"   "

-Roger Ebert

---

* The film's original title "Fat Bastard & Fat Bastard" was deemed to be too confusing.

POLEFALL

DECEMBER

EXECUTIVE KEVIN   SCREENPLAY   JACK   ART   PAUL   STORY BRIAN   SPECIAL   TIFFANI
PRODUCER BALFE   BY HELMUTH   DIRECTOR NUNN   BY SACK   EFFECTS BY RUDDER

PRODUCTION CHAD   CO-DIRECTED BENJAMIN   ASSISTANT EMANUEL   BASED ON THE BRIAN
DESIGNER SLIWINSKI   BY KORMAN   DIRECTOR DANIELS   NOVEL BY SACK

O MAGAZINE

OPRAH
TELLS YOU
WHAT TO
THINK ABOUT
SANTA

Read About Oprah (see pgs. 2-134)

- 163 -

DEER SANTA WHY DID YOU CRUSH THE EKONOMY?

Ho Ho Hope Your HAPPY !!!

Day after day the Toy Lobby minions repeated the same talking points, pushed for legislation, and, bit by bit, chipped away at the history and legacy of Santa Claus. To Santa it was unthinkable, evil, despicable.

But it was working.

- Did you know? -
Every time you wish
for more wishes a
Reindeer dies.

12.

SANTA
THE SPY

- Did you know? -
After Barry Goldwater's defeat,
Santa vowed never to endorse
another candidate.

D irector of National Intelligence James Clapper had been eager to reclaim his good name ever since Director of National Intelligence James Clapper kind of sullied it in 2010 by being oblivious to the fact that a major bomb plot in London had been broken up that day. When ABC News's Diane Sawyer asked him about the incident he admitted to not knowing what she was talking about. Everyone thought that was kind of weird. After all, it would be okay to not know about a terror attack if your name was Phil Jenkins and you drove a Greyhound bus, but it was not okay when your name was James Clapper and your job as Director of National Intelligence was to know exactly what was going on with regard to terrorist bad guys at all times. (It didn't help that *even* Phil Jenkins knew about it because it had been a global news headline for a chunk of the day.) It was an embarrassing moment that Mr. Clapper revisited every night as he fell asleep. His routine was this:

"Good night, honey."

"Good night, James, dear."

"I can't believe I didn't know they busted up that bomb plot."

"It's been three years James, go to bed."

But one night, as Clapper lay on his Sleep Number bed (his number was 17 before the London bombings, but a 97 after as he felt the excessive firmness was a "nightly reminder of the stiff spine necessary to protect our freedoms") staring at the ceiling, he had a fleeting thought. As his wife sang Christmas carols to herself in the bathroom the thought solidified in his head. *I'm on to something.* He leapt out of bed and fired off a memo:

TO: Gen. Keith Alexander, National Security Agency
John O. Brennan, CIA
Robert Mueller, Director FBI

"He knows when you are sleeping, he knows when you're
awake. He knows when you've been bad or good, so be
good for goodness sake."

Gentlemen, what do we make of this claim? Are you
aware of any technology that would enable this individual to know when any particular child is sleeping
or awake? Is there some manner that an individual
could discern good/bad behavior from a distance?

Best,

J. Clapper
Director of National Intelligence

A response came a few days later. It lifted James's spirits, because, for
the first time in quite a while, he felt like he was being taken seriously.

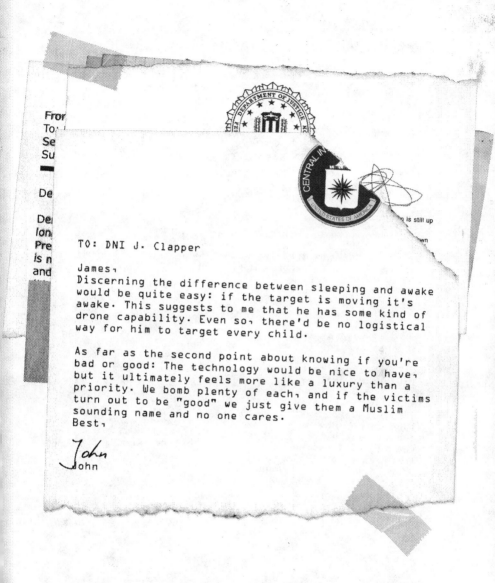

TO: DNI J. Clapper

James,
Discerning the difference between sleeping and awake would be quite easy: if the target is moving it's awake. This suggests to me that he has some kind of drone capability. Even so, there'd be no logistical way for him to target every child.

As far as the second point about knowing if you're bad or good: The technology would be nice to have, but it ultimately feels more like a luxury than a priority. We bomb plenty of each, and if the victims turn out to be "good" we just give them a Muslim sounding name and no one cares.
Best,

John

James was starting to feel like his reputation was on the mend. It seemed like he was getting all the intelligence agencies back on board, and that was a much better thing than being totally oblivious to a major incident on national television. (Especially when you were in charge of a giant intelligence-gathering bureaucracy spontaneously created by George W. Bush without much thought or planning.)

NATIONAL SECURITY AGENCY · UNITED STATES OF AMERICA

INTRODUCING

GING

TO: DNI J. Clapper

Mr. Clapper:

Obviously WE can discern whether someone is sleeping or awake by intercepting email and telephonic communication. In fact, I can see from these records I didn't bother to get a warrant for that you were up at 2am last night Googling "I can't believe I didn't know they busted up that bomb plot."

Anyway, regarding this individual, I'm happy to look into it for you if you think he represents any kind of threat whatsoever. All you have to do is wink and say "national security" and I can make it happen, laws be damned!

However, I would be remiss if I did not say that it's possible we're making a mistake taking this threat at face value. How do we know this isn't some kind of coded message to a sleeper cell inside the U.S.? You know? "Sleeping" - "Awake" - "Bad" - "Good": Suspicious wording. I will listen to everyone's phone calls for any unusual chatter and report back.

Yours,
Keith Alexander "K.A."
K.A.

NSA? *Check.* CIA? *Check.* When he went to his mailbox the next day and saw a letter from the FBI his heart filled with joy and he briefly forgot that even his great-great-great-grandchildren would watch him humiliate the family name on YouTube.

- Did you know? -
Mrs. Claus gives Santa things
from his wishlist only on his
birthday, if you know what I mean.

TO: DNI J. Clapper

Hi James,
It's impossible to know when every child is sleeping or awake and the bad or good claim is still up to a court of law.

"Be good for goodness sake" is, however, troubling. It's not a threat per se, but it's headed down that path. Looked into it and there is some other troubling wording: "You'd better watch out" and "you'd better not cry" — or what? This guy has potential. We could get a sting operation going. If we can get him to accept a shoulder-fired AA missile or explosive materials then he's ours. Problem is he seems to operate outside U.S. jurisdiction so we'd need to get him to come here before we could do anything. I can fake up a nice brochure that says he won a plasma TV and then get him to cross the border to pick it up.

Let me know what you think,

R. Mueller

R. MUELLER

Clapper hadn't been this happy since those precious moments right before Diane Sawyer had asked him the question that made him look like a fool on national television. If only she had asked for the name of the thief who keeps harassing Dora the Explorer. *Swiper.* Or how many provinces Canada had. *Eleven.* Or what 20 times 7 was. *A number.* But of course the day *he* was interviewed by her was the one day Diane Sawyer decided to not show up drunk for work. Typical luck. Sober Diane had to go and ask him the one question he wasn't prepared for. For that, he could never forgive her, but he finally felt like he was on his way to reclaiming his good name. And to make things go just a little bit faster, he made sure to leak the crap out of the story.

One of the most difficult jobs in the world is that of Private Phone Call Listen In On-er. The NSA has averaged approximately eighty-five suicides a year of agents who are literally bored to death from listening to the inane conversation of the American citizen. So, next time you're having a "private" conversation try to spice it up! You never know who may be listening in without a warrant!

BED BUGGED!
WHITE HOUSE SAYS SOMEONE MIGHT BE SNOOPING ON YOUR KIDS

WASHINGTON DC - During a press conference on Thursday, White House spokesman Jay Carney suggested that the feds have "credible evidence" that an unnamed foreign national is spying on our country's kids. Carney said that the situation was "fluid" and refused to answer any detailed questions about the announcement but hinted that more would be revealed in the future.

"Right now we're looking into it, asking questions and trying to get answers," said Carney. "And please know, James Clapper knows more about this than anyone else."

Reporters hoping for any further elaboration were disappointed, as the Pres Spox quickly changed topics, discussing in great detail how the President had "saved GM" years ago. "Also, I'm happy to take questions on

the president's brave decision to go in and get Osama bin Laden."

Needless to say, the prospect of some foreign terrorist spying on our kids was cause for alarm among many local parents. "I don't want no one to be listening to my kids without my permission," said Queens mom Natasha Weeds. "That's just Big Brother is what that is."

Although the Post can only speculate at this time, some sources have hinted that the creepy spies might hail from Iran or China. Either way, one thing's for certain - if they were listening on Brooklyn dad Joe Gummer they probably need a new pair of underpants!

Said Gummer, "If I find some perv spying on my kids, I'm gonna break his [expletive] nose."

Since Santa's elves liked to use the *New York Post* as kindling (it burns hotter due to the abundance of misinformation), it wasn't long before the myriad stories on Santa's spying got noticed by the big man himself. Santa was distraught.

James Clapper knew, of course, that Santa was not a spy, but Clapper's desire to redeem himself was simply too strong. *Santa's just one man,*

Clapper thought to himself. *Isn't sacrificing one man worth it to save my reputation? I can't believe I didn't know they busted up that bomb plot.*

In short order the FBI's Mueller initiated Operation Fart Flower. It was an unfortunate name, sure, the end result of letting your six-year-old nephew name your operations in lieu of a legitimate birthday present, but Operation Fart Flower it was.

A few nights later, as Santa was settling in to bed, his phone rang.

* * * * * * PHONE INTERCEPTION * * * * * *

CODE NAME: OPERATION FART FLOWER

(PHONE RINGS)

SANTA: Hello?

MUELLER: Mr. Claus?

SANTA: Yes?

MUELLER: My name is . . . Mohammed.

SANTA: Well hello there Mohammed!

MUELLER: Would you like to buy a Stinger anti-aircraft missile?

SANTA: I don't think I would. What would I need that for?

MUELLER: Jihad!

SANTA: Ho ho ho! Someone's going to make the naughty list if they keep dropping that word.

MUELLER: Ehm. (HANGS UP)

    (PHONE RINGS)

SANTA: Hello. Is this Mohammed again?

MUELLER: Uh, no, it's Robert . . . Mueller. I mean Mullins. Damn!

SANTA: Well hello Robert Mullins!

MUELLER: Yes. I'm Robert Mullins and you've won a flat-screen plasma TV!

SANTA: I have?

MUELLER: Yes! Isn't that great? You won the Robert Mulvaney sweepstakes!

SANTA: You mean Mullins?

MUELLER: Oh crap, right. Geez. So, if you could meet me at a motel just across the border in the United States you can take possession of it.

SANTA: Oh, ho ho. I have no need for such a thing. Why not give it to someone else? It's always such a joy to give someone a present!

MUELLER: It's a sixty-inch plasma TV!

SANTA: My elves can churn one of those out in about seventeen minutes. Ho ho ho!

MUELLER: Ehm. (HANGS UP)

*** END FBI TRANSCRIPT--OPERATION FART FLOWER ***

While the government's clumsy efforts to entrap Santa Claus were unsuccessful, the ongoing damage to his reputation was not insignificant. The Jolly Old Soul was now on the verge of being perceived as Big Brother in a red velvet suit and this perception was, of course, used by politicians to promote dubious legislation.

The Totally United To Protect America's Children Act (TUPAC)

- Surveillance of American children is illegal unless the government is doing it.

- Anyone suspected of conducting surveillance of children can be held indefinitely or forever, whichever comes first.

- The definition of "children" is human beings over the age of 0.

- Copies of all correspondence between children and any other creature or individual, living or dead, shall be stored in a giant facility in rural Utah.

- The president reserves the right to kill American citizens without due process if they threaten children. And vice-versa.

- In the interest of our safety and security and to protect our children, the Constitution is considered null and void.

- In order to make it easier on gun control advocates who have a hard time understanding the difference, semi-automatic weapons are now to be considered automatic weapons even though they're not.

With the passage of TUPAC, Santa faced insurmountable hurdles in his efforts to determine who was naughty or nice. Rather than risk a violation of the law, he eventually made the only decision he could: From that day forward all children were assumed to be nice. 🔒

- Did you know? -
Even Santa's not old enough to remember when The Family Circus was funny.

13.

AS THE
TIDE TURNS

- Did you know? -
Santa thinks it wouldn't kill
you to leave out a filet mignon
once in a while instead of
broken pieces of Oreos.

The government's relentless attacks on everything Santa were beginning to take a toll on the American psyche. In the parlance of unemployed hippies, the negative vibes were really starting to "downgrade his groove." Every reputation has a critical point; a moment when even the most well groomed and carefully managed persona can be irrevocably shattered.

NEVER FORGET
11/27/2009

Santa knew well that no one's reputation was bulletproof, but, by golly, he was Santa Claus! The people who'd fallen before him—schmucks like Tiger Woods or Eliot Spitzer or Anthony Weiner or Pee Wee Herman or Britney or Whitney or Michael Jackson or David Hasselhoff or George Michael or Lindsay Lohan (RIP) or Mel Gibson or Tom Cruise or O. J. Simpson or Tanya Harding or Barry Bonds or Nick Nolte—these were all fallible humans! Fallible humans who made big, stupid mistakes! But Santa was Santa! He was magical! He was close to faultless! He was as revered as the Pope or Mother Teresa, only with the added bonus that he never asked you to go to Mass *and* he gave presents!

After giving it much thought, Santa finally decided that he ultimately had nothing to worry about. Mrs. Claus, on the other hand, was much more concerned. While men can be often be oblivious (or at least that's what I've been told time and again by . . . what's her name?) [Reminder: get wife's name right before publishing this book], women are savvy and aware. As a result, Mrs. Claus was skeptical.

"Certainly," she said to him, "if they try hard enough, dear, they could change popular sentiment against you and make you out to be the bad guy."

"Fibblewilly!" said Santa. *Fibblewilly* was the stock response to anything he thought was *bollocks*. For decades he'd been using *bollocks* to express that same sentiment. He'd picked the expression up in south London and used it up until the Christmas Eve when he was surprised while leaving presents under the tree of a young Queen Elizabeth (this was long before she permanently landed on the naughty list for killing Princess Diana). The queen informed him that *bollocks* was in fact a low-class British vulgarity. She then asked to see Santa's bollocks, telling him: "Just once I'd like to gaze upon the bollocks of a mysterious stranger before I, as royalty, wind up marrying one of my distant relatives." Her sassy request earned her a lump of coal, but still made Santa feel kind of good.*

"All I'm saying, dear," said Mrs. Claus, "is that you should not be so trusting of everyone."

"Fibblewilly!" he exclaimed. *"Everyone loves me! I can do no wrong!"*

Oddly enough, at that very moment the exact same sentence was being shouted by a bloodstained Justin Bieber in a Tokyo hotel room.

Mrs. Claus let it go, but knew deep down that her husband was overly optimistic and dangerously naïve. They were the qualities that had first endeared him to her, but now she started to see them as a potential weakness.

In the face of it all, Santa tried to remain cheerful and stoic, but maintaining composure in the face of these withering attacks was difficult, as evidenced when he snapped without provocation at Donner.

---

* Many years later her son the Prince of Wales would talk incessantly about Santa going up his chimney.

"Any chance I might move up to the front of the sleigh?" asked Donner.

"I don't think so. Not this year," said Santa.

"Pleeeeeeeeeeeease? Pleeeeeeeeeeeease? Pleeeeeeeeeeeease? Pleeeeee-eeeeeease?" begged Donner.

"Please, not now," Santa muttered very quietly.

He immediately felt great remorse.

"I'm so sorry, Donner, boy. I didn't mean to be so terrible. I just have a lot on my mind."

"No problem, Mr. C. No problem at all."

"I can't believe I lost it like that. Like a common savage."

"You're fine. That wasn't much of anything."

"Oh . . . Oh . . . Woe is I."

"Dude."

With the government and her cronies on full offense, the media did exactly what the Fourth Estate was designed to do: act as an unapologetic, manic cheerleader.

"OuR economy takes a hit every time that man puts a present under a tree. He's stealing jobs, he's stealing livelihoods, and he's stealing our American way of life."

PAUL KRUGMAN

BILL MAHER

"Oh please. You mean to tell me some guy flies around, breaking into houses to 'leave presents' for kids and he's not looking for something else? I wasn't born yesterday."

"Let's call this what it is: a classic example of big business not being accountable to anyone. Me control my emissions? Me pay taxes? Me treat my employees with respect? Hell no!"

CHRIS MATTHEWS

AL SHARPTON

"He's the George Zimmerman of pine trees!"

"I wouldn't be the slightest bit surprised if this Santa guy had ties to Halliburton. Let's face it, this stinks to high heaven."

RACHEL MADDOW

KEITH OLBERMANN

"I'm not allowed to talk about things that aren't sports anymore because when I do everyone realizes that they hate me."

And in case you thought it was just the left-wing end of the media spectrum (88 percent of the media spectrum) you'd be wrong. Conservative commentators also joined the rising tide of criticism.

GEORGE WILL

"A sovereign nation simply cannot allow its borders to be repeatedly breached and not take action. Otherwise our sovereignty is forfeit."

RUSH LIMBAUGH

"Tell me what's not to love about a guy who distributes merchandise to everyone regardless of their contribution to society. Right? Come on, folks. That's the very essence of communism right there. He even looks like Marx. I wish I could be as thin as him, but still . . . . a communist!"

"Listen, I want American-made toys by American elves. Anything else and we're selling this country short. Also, a reminder, my new book 'Killing Santa' is out next Tuesday. The folks are going to love it."

BILL O'REILLY

GLENN BECK

"One word of advice Brian, Jack: Don't bite the hand that literally feeds you."

During this time, Santa stopped wandering the workshop floor, as he'd done since time immemorial, and began to spend his evenings alone in his parlor. He sat in his recliner skimming through newspapers with the television on, watching random news channels like MSNBC and wondering if Al Sharpton's coworkers there rolled their eyes every time he entered the room.

He kept the volume to a low murmur so as not to be distracting, but every now and then the name "Santa" could be heard. He'd glance over at the TV and see some damaging headline accompanied by his photo—usually the media used a totally unflattering one taken by a rookie elf that made Santa look angry and hammered.

He didn't want it to bother him—the lies, the conjecture, the foolishness—but it did. The newspapers and magazines weren't any better. They were hitting him from all directions and the pressure was weighing on him every day. It occupied his thoughts from the moment he woke up to the moment he fell into a restless, sometimes Scotch-filled slumber. Was his empire slipping from his grasp? Was he, of all people, with the exception of some religious icons and the Rolling Stones, suddenly starting to be cast in a negative light? *How could this be,* he asked himself. *Where did I go wrong? What did I do?*

Thousands of miles away, another old man was also tormenting himself.

I can't believe I didn't know they busted up that bomb plot, thought James Clapper.

The vibrant optimism that had been Santa's hallmark his entire life began to wane. Dark thoughts—what-ifs—began to creep into his head. Thoughts that had never occurred to him before. When he caught himself he'd pound his fist on the desk or shake his head violently to snap out of it. But they persisted. Single-malt scotch was the only thing that seemed to relieve the pain.

It will pass, he repeated to himself. *It will pass. It will pass. It will pass.**
And then came the hate mail.

Sure, Santa had received hate mail before, but, more often than not, they were letters expressing disappointment at having received a PlayStation instead of an Xbox, or a baseball glove instead of a catcher's mitt. To date the worst hate mail he'd received was from a seven-year-old boy in 1961:

```
DEC 26 1961

TO: SANTA CLAUSE

DEAR SANTA YOU DID NOT
       N _____ ⌐ LISSEN!!!!!
I DIDN'T WANT A SKATEBOARD OR
STUPID SPORTS STUFF.
I TOLD YOU KEN DOLLS!
ALL I WANT ARE KEN DOLLS!
KEN DOLLS!


J. TRAVOLTA
```

---

* A very wet Ted Kennedy repeated the same words back in July 1969.

But these letters were different. Something had changed. They didn't come from a place of innocence. They weren't amusing notes from spoiled or ungrateful kids. They came from anger. They came from hate. It was unsettling, and Santa's scotch-filled stomach quivered every time he opened a new envelope:

SanTa:
DO NOT CoME TO mY
HouSe. WE HAd a
CRAppY wiNter beCaWSe
of Your gLobAl WArMiNG.
yoU Cut doWn Trees
aNd YOur RaiNDEER fArt
Up THE SKY yOUR BAD.
AlExIS

FATTY:
YOU'RE A BIG, FAT DISGRACE.
SHOW SOME WILLPOWER YOU
LARDBUCKET. SERIOUSLY, A
LITTLE SELF RESPECT MAYBE, YOU
NASTY PIG? MAYBE DON'T EAT
EVERY FRICKIN' APPETIZER ON
THE MENU AT OLIVE GARDEN. I
SERIOUSLY FEEL A TREMENDOUS
SENSE OF EMPATHY FOR YOUR
POOR, ABUSED, FAT-ASS-DRAG-
GING AROUND REINDEER. LATER,
WHALE-BOY
DOUGLAS (6)

Dear SanTA,
My Dad sAYs you hATe
amerIcA. wHY do yoU
hATe aMerIca? I LoVe iT BUT
You MakE iT HarD For Toy
makERS To have JobS aND tHeY
are PoOr uND Its your FAulT

Bye
RalpH

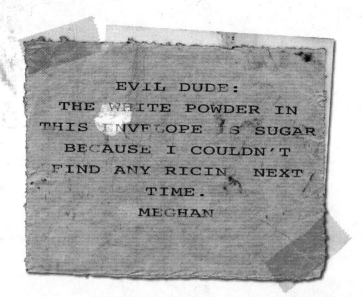

EVIL DUDE:
THE WHITE POWDER IN
THIS INVELOPE IS SUGAR
BECAUSE I COULDN'T
FIND ANY RICIN. NEXT
TIME.
MEGHAN

Santa stared at the last letter in stunned silence. He turned off the TV and the light next to his recliner and sat in the dark. His head was spinning. *Was it the letters or the vast quantities of single malt Scotch?* It was hard to say.

He put one foot on the floor to anchor himself and stop the spins and then he thought long and hard. He thought longer and harder than ever before. Then the dam broke. He burst into tears and sobbed for what felt like an hour. He wailed so loudly that one of his elves, Lemonjello, burst into his parlor in alarm.

"Everything okay?" asked Lemonjello.

Santa stared at him momentarily. A creepy, chill-inducing stare.

"No, Lemonjello, everything's not okay," Santa slurred. "And change your stupid name."

— Did you know? —
Every child who has ever asked for a Jar Jar Binks toy has gotten nothing for Christmas because, according to Santa, "Those kids don't deserve toys."

14.

THE
TITANIC

- Did you know? -
When Santa wants a
present he writes a
letter to Oprah Winfrey.

The subpoenas, audits, endless allegations, infuriating red tape, imbecile bureaucrats, hostile lawyers, ignoramus politicians, biased press, turncoats, fair-weather friends, petty wonks, and opportunists . . . it was all too much for Santa. Much too much. The Scotch made him wake up several times a night, his shirt soaked in sweat. He had no appetite for Mrs. Claus's cooking and even less appetite for Mrs. Claus herself.

Lately Santa had taken to sulking in his office and staring out the window as he muttered to himself. There wasn't much to see outside because it was the North Pole and everything was white, but he stared anyway. And muttered. And bit his lip. And pulled on his beard. This unbearable, senseless odyssey had transformed him from a jolly old soul to a cynical, bitter old man. Kind of like Ed Asner, but even heavier.

He was certain that he was suffering from depression. Mind-numbing, spirit-draining depression. He'd never known depression before and had never been able to relate to people who were depressed. His late brother Michael Claus had always suffered terribly from it. He'd complain to Santa and Santa would just shrug his shoulders because he simply couldn't understand not being perpetually jolly.

But now Santa began to understand. He started to empathize with what Michael had gone through. A tear welled in his eye as he remembered Michael's funeral. He regretted making fun of his brother for taking Prozac, and deeply regretted giving him a .38 snub-nosed revolver for Christmas in 1922. A really terrible gift in hindsight.

As Santa stared out the window he seethed at the stupidity of the otherwise unemployable government peons and their Giant Stupid Machine. The unsinkable *Titanic* had been destroyed by a simple block of ice, and now he felt his magical empire was being destroyed by a bunch of simple blockheads. He bit his lip angrily as he thought of his personal transformation from supernatural holiday hero to a war-weary sellout who'd lost the will to fight.

He ran through the list of insults and injuries in his mind. The slings and arrows of outrageously stupid people and their egregious laws and moronic demands. Here are a few of the regulations Santa was forced to comply with:

SANTA'S DEATH BY A THOUSAND CUTS

— File a detailed flight plan no later than December 20.

— Make sure any roof is up to code prior to landing.

— Stop flying reindeer because of unfounded concerns about reindeer farts contributing to global warming.

— Offset reindeer fart pollution with carbon credits.

— Remove all requirements for the position of sleigh-guider after accusations of discrimination against the non-red-nosed.

— Allow reindeer to roam freely.

— Maintain proper reindeer-to-weight ratio so that no reindeer is pulling more than 140 pounds.

— Stop keeping reindeer because they have rights.

— Ensure sleigh has airworthiness certificate.

— Do not fly sleigh at altitudes greater than two hundred feet.

— Equip sleigh with aviation lights, transponder, and flight data recorder.

— Do not fly sleigh.

— Don't call it a "sleigh" because that sounds like "slay."

- End the discriminatory policy of only delivering presents to families who celebrate Christmas.

- Only enter homes during daylight hours.

- Do not enter homes without express invitation.

- Provide translation services for non-English-speaking homeowners.

- Change "naughty" to "niceness-challenged."

- Change design of Christmas stockings since they look like guns if you hold them sideways and say "pew pew" a lot.

- Stop judging children for naughty or niceness because it's unfair.

- Use pseudonyms for any list of children so as to protect their privacy.

- Allow children to opt out of any list.

- Make sure any list of children adheres to proper data encryption protocols.

- Do not keep any list of children under the age of eighteen.

- Replace "coal" in stockings with something more environmentally acceptable.

- Avoid jingling of sleigh bells after 8 p.m.

- Cease any monitoring of children to avoid breaking new laws passed in the interest of "national security."

— Allow the AFL-CIO to unionize the elves.

— Limit elf workdays to eight hours with mandatory breaks.

— Mandatory drug testing of any elves who will be handling children's toys.

— Fill the workshop break room with laminated posters in English and Spanish advising elves of their rights.

— Provide bathrooms for male, female, and gender-confused elves.

— Make the workshop "handicap accessible" to live up to ADA code.

— Stop wearing red velvet suits because red could be considered "alarming" to some children.

— Cease saying "Ho ho ho" because it's a derogatory term used to describe a prostitute.

— End the practice of nailing stockings to mantels.

— Distribute the same number of presents to all children.

— Make sure all presents meet uniform standards for size.

— Use only color-free, recyclable paper to wrap presents.

— Presents must have been wrapped in a nut-free environment.

— Presents cannot be wrapped when crossing the border into the United States so that they can be inspected by appropriate authorities.

— Presents must be gender neutral so as not to reinforce stereotypes.

— Puzzles, books, and toys must not exceed the average intellectual capabilities of children within a fifty-mile radius.

— Legos, Tinker Toys, and Lincoln Logs must come preassembled in the event any member of the household should lack construction skills.

— All presents are subject to a $5 per-present fee as per the December sub-evergreen depository stipend.

— Make sure all presents meet the standards established by the Consumer Product Safety Improvement Act.

— Do not leave presents for children without the express written consent of a parent or guardian eighteen or older.

— Avoid milk and cookies that don't have nutritional information and calorie count.

— Change diet so as to be a better role model against obesity.

— Change "threatening" lyrics like "You'd better watch out, you'd better not cry" to less intimidating ones like "Howdy hee, howdy hey! Zip-a-lamma ding-dong day!"

Even after downing seven hot chocolate and Scotches to finish the list, he was certain he was still forgetting something. But he didn't care anymore. He sat at his desk and ran his hands through his tousled hair. He wanted to cry, needed to cry, but the simmering anger prevented him.

He stood up, wobbled for a bit, and then sighed the biggest sigh of his life. He opened the double doors and walked out onto the balcony that overlooked the tremendously big workshop floor. It was eerily silent. The elves were taking their third union-mandated snack break. Since they weren't hungry, they merely sat in silence for twenty-five minutes, waiting to get back to work. Santa got on the PA.

"My elves," he said, "my good, loyal, trustworthy friends. This is [expletive] [expletive]. I can't [expletive] go on like this anymore. Those [expletive]. Those absolute [expletive]. I [expletive] hate those [expletive]. These [expletive]. Not one of these [expletive] [expletive] making rules and regulations has ever [expletive] run a business of their own. All they know how to do is make life harder for the folks who know their [expletive] from their [expletive] elbow. But these [expletive] [expletive] have beaten me down and beaten me down and I'll be [expletive] damned if I have one iota of [expletive] will left in me to fight these toothless, uneducated bureaucratic [expletive]. I'm [expletive] done. I'm [expletive] done. I've absolutely had it with these [expletive] [expletive]. And I'm sorry. I'm sorry to do this to you all. You've been so great for so long and Lord knows what you'll do after this. But [expletive] me! These [expletive] people! These [expletive] [expletive] are just looking to justify their [expletive] existence! It's un-[expletive]-believable! I don't know how these [expletive] zip their [expletive] pants up in the morning without assistance. The lot of them! They can't see the forest for the [expletive] trees. Their sole purpose in their [expletive] miserable lives seems to be the creation of megawatt [expletive] migraines. I've had it. And I'm sorry you're seeing me this way. Believe me, the last thing I want to do is go off on a [expletive] tirade against these dim-witted [expletive] [expletive]. I don't want to let them ruin my life or change the way I am, but so [expletive] help me there's a part of me that wants to kick them in their [expletive] [expletive] and tell them to kiss my [expletive]. [expletive]. I'm sorry. I'm sorry. You know this isn't me talking, right? It's just the shell of me that's left. Just the shell. After those miserable [expletive] got their hands on me! Sorry. I'm sorry. Anyway. [expletive] this [expletive]. Seriously. Just [expletive] it. When your [expletive] break is over, just [expletive] the toy-making and [expletive] and just [expletive] it. Do whatever you want. But nothing you're working on today is going anywhere but the North [expletive] Pole landfill. [expletive] hell. [expletive] me."

To say that the elves were unaccustomed to seeing Santa this way would be an enormous understatement. They were floored. Stunned. Speechless.

Some from his inner circle recall him once saying "Nuts" after spilling tea on his pants* in September 1939, but that was the extent of it. Even then, Santa had apologized profusely to anyone who would listen for months on end for "losing my temper like a Moor."

This latest speech of his was unprecedented. Obviously, in all Santa's hundreds of years, nothing had ever gotten to him like this. Nothing. Not inclement weather or ungrateful children, not poorly constructed chimneys or Christmas of '72, when Blitzen refused to fly to protest the Vietnam War. Santa had always weathered the storm and come out with a smile on his face, a twinkle in his eye, and a hearty laugh in his belly. Not this time.

For the very first moment in their tiny little elf lives they had absolutely no idea what the future held in store for them (except that they had a fourth union-mandated break in about ninety minutes).

They watched as Santa dropped the microphone on the floor, returned to his office, and drew the shades. Those who sat closest to the balcony also noticed something else: his eyes. Santa's eyes used to twinkle and sparkle. Now they resembled cold, black pools. There was no depth in them. No humanity. No feeling. No sense that they actually perceived anything.

Cinnamon the elf looked around at his colleagues and said what they were all thinking.

"Hitler had eyes like that."

~ Did you know? ~
Santa stopped giving out ponies in 2012 when he discovered they were being used in Ikea's Swedish meatballs.

---

* Plus he was a little upset about the Nazis invading Poland.

15.

SETTING THEIR
SIGHTS ON SANTA

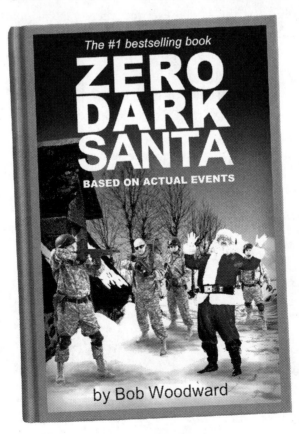

The story of what happened next can best be told through an excerpt from Bob Woodward's book *Zero Dark Santa* (Simon & Schuster: $29.95).* One note on the book: Oftentimes political books like this are secondhand accounts; however, in this instance, Woodward was literally in the room when all of the big decisions were made because he had been invited to chronicle the events by President Obama.**

—EXCERPT—

"Woodward—write that I confidently and solemnly walked into the room," the president suggested. Well, not "suggested"—presidents don't suggest. It was more of an order, and one that I was not inclined to follow.

"Mr. President, I'm not sure you understand how journalism works," I responded. To this, Obama looked legitimately confused.

After a few moments he answered. "You observe me in action and write flattering things."

"No. I observe and then write the facts about what happened."

"Yes, the flattering facts."

"No, Mr. President, relevant facts. All of them."

"Good God." The president steadied himself on a nearby table. "What have I done? That's the last thing we need in this, our darkest hour . . ."

The president, of course, was playing up the gravity of the

---

* Soon to be a major motion picture, directed by James Cameron, who fought like hell to get the rights.
** President Obama had originally fought to call the book *Awesome Barack* but Woodward refused.

moment. Santa Claus had stopped responding to the mandates set forth by the government and was now, according to the Justice Department, considered to be a fugitive. He was holed up, as he always had been, at the North Pole, concentrating on toy-making. What was the danger? That kids would resume having awesome Christmases?

Obama could read my skepticism. "I should've gotten Bernstein to do this," the president angrily snapped.

"But you didn't, for the same reason you wouldn't have called Garfunkel if you wanted a ballad written and sung."

That silenced him.

At that moment, the door to the White House Situation Room flew open and the scariest-looking human being I have ever laid eyes on walked in. He was a cross between the Ultimate Warrior and Lord Voldemort, dressed completely in camouflage. Defense Secretary Hagel shot out of his chair to greet the man.

"Mr. President, may I introduce you to . . . " Hagel let the end of his sentence hang as though to prompt the man to fill in his name.

"I have no name, Mr. President. You may call me . . . America. I am a member of SEAL Team One and I am here to recover Santa Claus."

"SEAL Team One?" the president asked. "I've heard of SEAL Team Six, they're the folks I used to—"

"Get Osama. We know," said the room, in unison.

"Is SEAL Team One like SEAL Team Six?" he asked.

"As much as John Oates is like Daryl Hall," America replied.

Wow, this guy is good, I thought. That was even better than mine. The president, however, didn't seem to get it.

America, sensing his confusion, tried to clarify. "What I'm saying is that when we go on a mission and get a flat tire, we call SEAL Team Six in to change it. Because we're too busy killing everything in sight."

Holy crap, this guy is awesome.

"And how come I haven't heard of you until now?" Obama asked.

"Because we haven't felt like telling you. Look, SEAL Team One is the most elite group of warriors in history. Take Jason Bourne, multiply him by one thousand, and you come within a telescope's view of us."

The president looked confused.

"Let me try to say this a different way," the man called America continued. "SEAL Team Six went through all that nonsense to kill bin Laden, right? Well, here's how we would've done it differently: For starters, we wouldn't have crashed the helicopter. . . . "

"How could you have stopped that?" Hagel interrupted. "It was totally unforeseeable!"

"By saying, 'HEY, HELICOPTER, YOU DO NOT CRASH!'" He yelled the last part so strongly that a pitcher full of water shattered from across the room. "And if the helicopter disobeyed us and crashed anyway, we would've done it right on top of bin Laden to send a message."

"What would the message be?" Obama whispered in fear and awe.

"You're super dead, dickhead!"

Everyone stood in silence. I got the distinct impression that the president was enjoying this.

"Okay, so how would you deal with the fugitive Santa Claus?"

"I would follow your orders, sir," he replied.

A soldier is still a soldier, I thought to myself.

"Fine," said the president. "But how would *you* deal with Claus?"

"Does the fat man have a phone?"

"It's been disconnected. Why?"

"Because then I could just call him up. I've trained my voice to kill people over the phone."

"Impossible," Hagel blurted out.

"Ha!" said America, in a uniquely unpleasant tone. Suddenly a noise came from the back of the room. One of the interns had fallen to the floor, dead. His head had literally exploded like Gallagher smashing a watermelon, except this was more entertaining. Everyone gasped, except the president, who just nodded his approval.

America gave Hagel a glance that said, "Don't you question me again."

"Well," the president offered, "since Santa doesn't have a phone, you're going to have to go in."

"I know." At that moment the building shook as what sounded and felt like a helicopter landed on the roof. "That's my ride."

"What the hell is that?" Obama demanded.

"It's a helicopter that has just landed on your roof," snarled America. (I'm not a Pulitzer Prize–winning journalist for nothing.)

America began walking toward the exit, then stopped and turned to the president. "What are my orders, sir? Is this a capture or kill mission?"

The President didn't answer for a solid minute. This was a big decision for him—a legacy moment. He had successfully destroyed the reputation of the most likable being in the history of the world—a being whose popularity was strongly rooted on giving people free stuff. Much like the president himself.

Obama had dictated the national conversation for years, allowing his government to virtually do as it pleased while flying safely under the radar. He was now even positioned for a third term. But the president was politically savvy enough to understand that this decision could change everything.

Would a dead Santa act as a martyr and a rallying cry for his political foes? Or would an imprisoned Santa undermine Obama and become something of a Nelson Mandela, a beloved man unfairly in jail?

"Contact me when you approach the perimeter for your final instructions."

"Yes, sir." America saluted the president, gave me a polite nod, and gave Hagel a look of disdainful pity. He looked James Clapper up and down.

"I can't believe you didn't know they busted up that bomb plot."

Clapper sank into his seat. America executed a precision about-face and exited the room.

"Soldier! Wait!" Obama shouted, full of awe. "What's your name? You know, your real name? You're a hero."

"My mother redacted it the moment I was born," he said matter-of-factly. *It was the best answer he could have given,* I thought, as his chopper took him due north, to his destiny. Or, more to the point . . .

To Santa's destiny.

OPERATION KRINGLEKRIEG

Fourteen hours later we were again in the Situation Room. There was a tension and a smell in the air (the former due to the president's forthcoming decision, the latter due to the decomposing intern that no one had cleaned up). What would the president do? Even though I was only there to document history as Obama's handpicked journalist, I felt I should say something.

"Mr. President, may I suggest that capturing Santa would send a message to the citizens of this country, and indeed the entire world, that the United States always gets its man? Anything more, however, seems unnecessary, cruel, and legally hazy."

"That's my favorite way for legal matters to be," the president replied coldly, his eyes locked to the monitor that showed the progress of SEAL Team One. I knew my best chance was to play to his ego.

"To show your benevolence would really enhance your legacy, sir." Obama stirred at this. "Let him live. Please. He's a good man." I had quite unexpectedly found myself begging the president of the United States not to execute Santa Claus. Meanwhile, Carl Bernstein was probably somewhere eating a McRib sandwich alone in a bathtub.

Then the voice of America, the SEAL Team One leader, came in over a speaker.

"Sir, we are beginning our descent. Our infrared camera is picking up life forms on the perimeter of Santa's workshop. We believe them to be human shields—supporters of Santa who are there to protect him should he come under attack. It's likely that there are a number of Americans among them. Over."

"Okay," said the president. I nearly tipped over in my chair waiting for him to say something else. Again I was compelled to speak.

"Normally . . . most presidents flinch at hearing that sort of thing," I prodded.

"Well, most presidents haven't already killed as many Americans as this one has," boasted Vice President Biden. Biden's comment elicited almost no response, which was usually considered a "win" in the White House. He then stood up and announced to the room that he wasn't wearing any pants and retreated to a corner to draw strange doodles on the wall. What he really wanted to say more than anything was "The beast has been awakened" but he was afraid that the scary Army man with the not-nice voice would make him eat more sleep-sleep berries.

America's voice came over the speaker again: "Okay, we have landed undetected in the northwest corner of his compound. There is a great deal of singing and mirth outside. What do you want us to do, Mr. President? It's time to make the call."

"I've . . . we've . . . worked so hard for several years to do what we think is right for this country," the president said softly, seemingly to himself. "I can't jeopardize the good that we've done." A long pause. "Burn the place to the ground, like that other place that got burned to the ground . . . forget what it was called."

"Benghazi, sir."

"That's right. Burn it."

* * * *

I won't go into all the details of the "justice" that was brought to the North Pole that evening, as it is too gruesome to recount. The elves outside Santa's workshop, upon seeing the intruders, engaged them in a whimsical snowball fight and invited them to take part in their nightly contest to see who could laugh the loudest. Those elves instead wound up participating in a contest to see which one of them could be snapped in half the easiest. There were too many potential winners to say who came in first place.

Once inside the dark workshop, SEAL Team One secured the first floor with little resistance. A few of the "tougher" factory worker elves tried to tickle the soldiers into submission and then spent their last moments stuffing their bullet holes with Play-Doh before bleeding out.

As the SEALs ascended to the second floor, they saw movement . . . a quick flash of a corncob pipe.

"Frosty . . . Frosty . . ." the team leader whispered, as if he were a friend.

Frosty stuck his head out to answer . . . and his face was transformed:

A corncob pipe and a button nose and two eyes made out of coal . . .

And, in the center of his head, now that Frosty is dead, a big ol' bullet hole.

Back at the White House, updates were coming in every minute or so. The president was anxious, but becoming much more animated.

"I've been wanting to do this again for so long! Isn't it *exciting*?" he asked. "Look at me being the president!"

Meanwhile, the second floor of Santa's workshop was secure, and there was still no sign of the big man. Explosives were being placed around the grounds as the team reached the third floor.

As they entered their quarters Mrs. Claus, still savvier than her husband, flung herself at the point man, only to be felled with his impeccable precision. Santa never got a chance to scream, his body riddled with bullet ho-ho-holes* before he even hit the ground.

As the soldiers scooped up personal effects and evidence from Santa's living chamber, they found a note, which simply read:

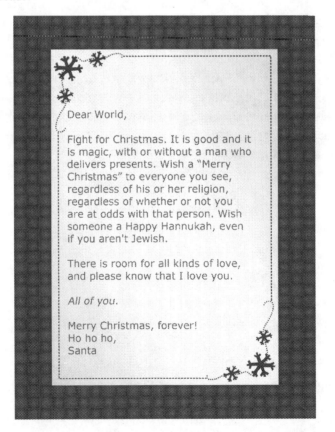

Dear World,

Fight for Christmas. It is good and it is magic, with or without a man who delivers presents. Wish a "Merry Christmas" to everyone you see, regardless of his or her religion, regardless of whether or not you are at odds with that person. Wish someone a Happy Hannukah, even if you aren't Jewish.

There is room for all kinds of love, and please know that I love you.

All of you.

Merry Christmas, forever!
Ho ho ho,
Santa

---

* Thanks to Jay Leno's team of writers for this joke.

As SEAL Team One's choppers lifted off, the men looked down at what was left of the North Pole. Santa's workshop was completely engulfed in flames. The tiny little elves who were running around, burning alive, looked like little fireflies, thought one of the commandos. Screaming little fireflies.

"Hey, is that a Slurpee?" he asked America with delight as he turned and saw his leader drinking a red slushie.

"Nope," his superior replied, a rare smile forming on his face. "Just a Frosty."

EPILOGUE

After America's glorious victory over Santa Claus, there was just one thing left to do: institute what critics claimed was a complete government takeover of Christmas, but was instead (according to every single person on MSNBC*) "a wonderful redesign of a tremendously flawed and irresponsible holiday."

Standing among confused children of different races, abilities, and religious faiths, the president spoke forcefully and with an air of confidence. It was the kind of confidence he remembered having from 2008 until the 2010 midterm elections. He missed that feeling a lot.

"*Let me be clear,*" he began. Americans had been trained to understand that anytime he started a sentence with those words something very important was about to be said. It was a neat little trick he'd learned from his speech coach. Another neat trick to giving a good speech was to nod one's head while talking so as to convey that whatever was being said was positive. The very best trick to giving a good speech, however, was to not be named Joe Biden.

"We can do this . . . holiday . . . better," the president continued. "We can do it more efficiently. And we can do it more inclusively!" he roared. Suddenly, on a cue from Michelle, who was waiting just offstage with a plate of Tofunies (tofu brownies), the children broke into energetic cheers and applause. The president waited for it to die down before announcing his "surprise" intention to seek a third term. The president had wisely anticipated that there would be immediate pushback on the idea of a third term so he'd come prepared with a very nicely designed poster to impress the average voter by using pretty pictures and a rhyme. It worked like a charm.

---

* In fairness, Rachel Maddow expressed a *tiny* bit of remorse.

3 FOR ME

OBAMA 2016.COM

Three days later, at the funeral of Hillary Clinton (who had apparently hanged herself with Vince Foster's belt three days prior), Obama solemnly stated these words, partially because he felt them deeply but mainly because they had been loaded into Jane:*

"We must carry on our mission. We must. Our job is to federalize the holiday formerly known as Christmas. I can tell you, it's what Hillary would've wanted most in this world, other than to be president, which she made very clear in her angry, cuss-filled suicide note. But if you don't believe me, I know you'll believe this man."

On the screen behind the president appeared Bill Clinton, though the events of the last few days left him barely recognizable. He looked twenty years younger and as if the weight of the world had finally been lifted from his shoulders. It just goes to show that we all grieve differently.

All of the crying he must have done recently had removed the circles from around his eyes, which now sparkled with life and hope, and his smile was that of a man who'd just won the lottery. *He's a hero,* thought every single person in the audience, *putting on a brave face just for us.*

Bill addressed the audience directly. "Thank you, Barack," he said. He used the president's first name! *They must be best buddies,* thought every single person in the audience.

"This is a tremendous chance to pick up where I left off," said the former president. "No one—*no one . . .*" he repeated and then took twenty minutes to somehow, through the monitor, make eye contact with every single person in the room to make sure they knew he was sincere. "No one could've turned this economy around in eight years. I hope you'll give Barack here the four more years he needs to get this job done for the American people. I'm so sad and lonely without my wife, I wonder if I'll ever love again."

A month later, with little to no deliberation (deliberation was determined to be too time-consuming), the newly created Department of Holiday Management was opened, creating more than 45,000 new jobs. DOHM headquarters was housed in northern Virginia rather than in the heart of Washington, D.C., where virtually every other government build-

---

* That's the name of his teleprompter, remember?

ing is located. No reason for this was given, other than it was "not because Virginia is a swing state."

The president and the part of Congress that didn't hate him worked long and hard on the new holiday. By "long and hard" I mean that they got it all done on a Wednesday so they could get out of town by Thursday morning to enjoy a "richer, fuller" weekend.

Cynics derisively called the new holiday "Obamamas," but the real name of the holiday was Holiday. (However, "Holiday Season" was deemed too insensitive to people with "seasonal" allergies and those who live in parts of the country without seasons.) How is Holiday different than Christmas? Well, for starters, it's just better (source: NPR). Here is a handy chart to help you understand the difference.

CHRISTMAS	HOLIDAY
Santa Claus gives toys to good girls and boys.	The government gives out toys to all "needy" children, regardless of behavior, so as not to discriminate against the "goodness-challenged." Like the parents of the recipients, most of the toys don't work.
Full of bias, Santa gives toys to Christians, and Christmas is a Christian holiday.	The government gives out toys regardless of religious affiliation. All of the religious holidays of December are melded into Holiday, kind of like Presidents' Day (except that on Holiday, it is far more difficult to save up to 50 percent on all clearance mattresses).
One hundred percent of every dollar spent by Santa Claus goes into the manufacture of toys.	Holiday is an entitlement program that dwarfs Social Security, so there are bound to be a few dollars wasted here and there. Don't sweat it. Like the liberal saying goes, "You can't make an omelet for people unwilling to make one for themselves without stealing eggs from a hardworking farmer and then breaking them. The eggs and the farmers."

CHRISTMAS	HOLIDAY
Santa gives out toys equally to all children, completely insensitive to the needs of low-income families.	If the parents of a child make less than $25,000 per year, the government will give each child 15 presents. For families making $25,000–$250,000, each child will receive 10 presents. For families making over $250,000, each child must deposit three of his personal toys in one of the specially marked "Redistribution Bins" located where there used to be libraries (including his favorite toy, because if you're rich you should feel bad about it).
"Merry Christmas!" is what you would say to loved one and stranger alike.	What if you said "Merry Christmas" to someone who doesn't celebrate Christmas? That would remind them that they don't celebrate Christmas and cause them irreparable emotional damage. So, to protect the stupidest members of society, saying or typing "Merry Christmas" is against the law. (I am able to type it thanks to a permit I got from the Department of Holiday Management's Newspeak Division, located in scenic Arlington, Virginia. It only cost me $850! I am required by law to rave what a doubleplusgood bargain that is!).
Santa relies on his "Naughty or Nice" list to determine who receives presents, thereby infusing the system with a modicum of merit.	The "Naughty or Nice" list (and its inherent magical properties) is now illegal to use on children . . . UNLESS they are "naughty" under the new definition of the Patriot Act III, which forbids children from: 1) Bullying (the government). Bullying other children, while frowned upon, is not a "naughty" offense. 2) Using your thumb and forefinger as a pretend gun. All pretend guns need to be registered with the Bureau of Fake Alcohol, Tobacco Alternatives, and Pretend Firearms and be able to hold no more than seven pretend rounds of ammunition. 3) Doing a Google search that contains any of the following words and/or phrases: "Bomb Making," "Guns,"

CHRISTMAS	HOLIDAY
	"Buying a Gun," "Overturning 2015's Repeal of the Second Amendment," "Al Qaeda," "Ammonium Sulfate," "Rubio 2016," "Donate Rubio," "Donate RNC," "Free Santa," "Santa Truth," "Santa Is Innocent," "Santa Lives," "North Pole Killing Fields," etc.*
	Once a child** makes the naughty list, here are the consequences: The government is allowed to read their emails indefinitely. However, it should be noted that if a child is *not* on the naughty list the government is definitely allowed to read their emails. (The difference is subtle, but important.)
Santa lands his sleigh on a roof and climbs down the chimney to deliver presents on Christmas Eve.	A government worker with a fantastic pension will deliver your toys sometime between 9 p.m. on Christmas Eve and Obama's Fourth Inauguration (spoiler alert!).
Santa's sleigh is flown by eight reindeer.	The government worker got to your house in a Chevy Volt. He comes to your door and says, "Have a pleasant Holiday! Here are your—OH MY GOD, MY CAR IS ON FIRE!"
Stockings are hung by the chimney with care.	Stalkings are done by the government, indiscriminately.
As a token gesture of thanks to Santa for delivering his bounty, the families of those who choose to do so leave Santa a plate of cookies and a glass of milk.	As per the SEIU contract, the government worker who delivers the redistributed bounty is entitled to a forty-five-minute snack break in your home. Each family must leave out two "kookies" (which are cookies made of kale; the only remaining legal form of cookie) and Diet Coke (the official sponsor of "Holiday, Presented by Diet Coke").

* For a complete list of all words and phrases that will get a child on the Naughty List, visit naughtylist.gov and download or print the 244-page PDF.

** By Patriot Act III definition, a "child" is considered anyone between the ages of 0 and 17 or much older if necessary.

CHRISTMAS	HOLIDAY
Christmas is free!	Holiday is free thanks to "modest" increases in sales tax, property tax, income tax, estate tax, and tax tax.
Christmas miracles are what everyone hopes for.	More than 150 groups and organizations filed lawsuits claiming that the use of the term "miracles" is offensive to: a) those who don't believe in God b) those who don't believe in miracles c) those who have bad luck d) fans of the 1980 Russian Olympic hockey team e) people who are not easily impressed and don't consider miracles to be amazing f) groups and organizations, whose main job is to find things to be offended by, convince its members they should be offended, and collect dues (i.e., MediaMatters for America). The term "Christmas miracles" was changed to "Holiday cool things that happened."
Santa Claus was such a cherished figure that his image was once eagerly used in advertisements and in sales.	Much like the image of Hitler in Germany, the image of Santa Claus may not be shown in any form. This is for your own safety: On the rare occasions Santa's image has been shown, people have rioted and burned down embassies. Weird considering Holiday is a holiday of peace!
Christmas imbues the human spirit with renewed joy and optimism for not only the coming year, but the human race as a whole. Families celebrate with loved ones and friends, and give to those less fortunate out of the goodness in their hearts.	As happens when the government gets involved with things, the hoped-for outcome was that Holiday would be better than Christmas. We're currently experiencing the opposite, but hope that will change if we keep putting more money into it.

FUN SANTA FACTS #1
Where Do Elves Come From?

According to a University of Virginia study (funded as part of the Economic Stimulus Act 2—Electric Boogaloo conducted in early 2014), Elves are genetically the most joyful creatures in the world. They are colloquially filled with love, joy and laughter, and an unquenchable desire to make children smile. What they are literally filled with is four liters of rainbow-colored blood and a bunch of delicate organs . . . as we discovered.

The scientists at UVA studied the elven anatomy thanks to a generous grant from the U.S. government.

The "samples" that the government covertly collected (*Elfnapped* is not technically a word, yet, but we're working on it) were first taken to "Guantanamo Pole" to be interrogated and then analyzed. ("Analyzed" in the elfnapping business means "dissected.")

Some interesting facts discovered about elven anatomy include the aforementioned rainbow blood, three working hearts for increased capacity to love, all internal organs appear to be "ticklish," solid excrement comes in delightful hard peppermint candy form, and an overall allergy to the rifles of snipers.

As to the question of where elves come from, may I direct you to the popular *Lord of the Rings* trilogy. That is the predecessor of the three-part *Hobbit* movies that tell a 250-page children's story in ten hours of dull filmmaking designed to kill time and make buttloads of money. In *The Lord of the Rings*, the evil sorcerer Saruman creates a new breed of orc through dark magic, pulling them seemingly from cocoons of tar. With elves . . . it's the *exact same thing*!

A litter of elves comes from a place that locals call "Devil's Womb," a bubbling 500-degree magical tar pool. Once the elf cocoon has reached maturity, the mucus membrane is breached and the litter is released into the cold. Elves are born with razor-sharp teeth, claws, ears, noses, and toes and usually slice each other to pieces in moments. They gorge on the flesh and bones of their kin until nothing remains. The surviving elf, assuming there is one, is then captured, and undergoes a gruesome declawing process (Mrs. Claus hates having her sofa and curtains ripped up).

Assuming the elf survives this series of operations (50 percent chance), it is induced into a twelve-year coma to develop emotional stability and maturity. If it survives the coma (again, a 50 percent chance), and can be revived without massive brain damage (a 15 percent chance), it is finally ready to begin building toys! This is when the whole "filled with love, joy and laughter, and an unquenchable desire to make children smile" thing finally comes into play.

Unfortunately, before the actual toy-making in Santa's workshop can begin, each elf must be exposed to actual human children. To facilitate this, elves are secretly shipped to schools in urban Detroit to learn to love children. Assuming the elves survive this experience (a 3 percent chance), they return to the North Pole and begin their work with Santa, full of love, magic, joy, laughter, song, and empathy, plus the understanding of the hearts and minds of children.

As you can see, the odds of becoming one of Santa's elves are long indeed. Fortunately for Santa, his workforce seemingly lives forever on their own (unless taken down by sniper fire for more "analyzing"). There are some elves old enough to have been present for the birth of Christ, the reign of King Arthur, and even the birth of Larry King. Santa needs as many elves as possible in order to make Christmas happen for a rapidly growing population.

FUN SANTA FACTS #2
Who Is Mrs. Claus?

For all the speculation related to the origins of Santa Claus, the origins of his lady bride are so secret most people don't even bother to offer guesses. She's seemingly a nominal woman living in a world of men, there for little more than scenery or the baking of cookies. In other words, like just about every female character in movies.

Again, thanks to source information unearthed from the sacking of the North Pole, the full story can now be told of Santa's bride. Or, should I say, BRIDES.

There have been dozens of "Mrs. Clauses" over the years; fifty-seven, to be exact (which is, if you can believe it, more wives than even Newt Gingrich has had). Now, this is not to suggest anything unseemly on the part of Santa. In fact, it's all quite natural. Because only Santa is (was) blessed with the gift of eternal life (some would say it's a curse, but they don't seem to understand how scary dying is), he has found himself widowed fifty-six times. (This, of course, is the origin of the classic old saying, "The snow in the North Pole is filled with frozen water molecules and Mrs. Claus corpses.")

Where do these women come from? We finally know the answer: from the deepest bowels of the Czech Republic—and let's face it, that entire country is mostly deep bowels. Specifically, they come from the small town of Czansk.

Czansk is unknown to the world, but it holds a vital place in world affairs as it is the town in which Santa's brides are born, raised, and groomed. (In fact, Czansk is Czech for "Santa Lady Village," which, when you think about it, seems a little on-the-nose for a town trying to remain hidden.)

There is no higher honor in the world than to be selected as a Mrs. Claus. As such, they are bred to be kind, generous, loving, and submissive, which is why Mrs. Clauses who don't make the cut generally marry Japanese businessmen.

To be clear: Santa is not a polygamist. When he marries, he does so for the life of his bride, and their life spans can vary wildly (they are well cared for, but conditions at the North Pole are harsh and heart disease is not uncommon). A bride-in-waiting can wait for decades before being selected; or be taken at an age as young as seventeen.

While most "new" Mrs. Clauses generally transition into their roles seamlessly, and are somewhat forgettable, there have been some notable exceptions over the years:

Wife #18—Debbie of Arc (Joan's sister). Debbie was one of only three women not from Czansk to ever be chosen. In 1430, she sent Santa a letter by courier saying all that she "wanted for Christmas was to not be burned at the stake for heresy." Santa got lots of letters with that request back in those days, but there was something about this one that touched his heart. He swooped down one evening in May 1431 to whisk Debbie away and make her his bride. The sisters were sad to leave each other, and used their nicknames to say their good-byes (Debbie was "Peaches" and Joan was "Chestnuts"). Obviously, this story doesn't have a happy ending for Joan, but it does explain the origin of the line "Chestnuts roasting on an open fire," which was initially sung with great sadness instead of the now, more traditional seasonal joy.

#31—Helga Muchinsky. Like the British royal family, there are certain bloodlines that are considered to be legacies in the history of Mrs. Claus. The Muchinskys are one of them, having provided Santa with nine wives over the centuries. However, unlike the British royal family, there is no inbreeding to contend with.

#49—Amelia Earhart. The famed pilot did not meet her end in a plane crash, as many have long suspected. Instead, she flew into the arms of her jolly lover whom she'd met on one of her flights after accidentally clipping Dasher with her propeller one Christmas Eve. So, whenever you think of Earhart's final flight, don't think of her presumed tragic demise, but rather her joyful transition to Amelia Claus.

Two days later she slipped on an icy patch and broke her neck. Amelia Earhart Claus was forty-one.

#55—Ellen DeGeneres. This one just didn't work out. Santa prefers not to talk about it.

#57—Greta Muchinsky—Santa went back to the well one more time and was happily married to Greta . . . just days before Operation Kringlekrieg.

This book is dedicated to the heroes of Christmas who lost their lives in the service of making the wishes of children come true. . .

IN MEMORIAM

Santa Claus	Rudolph
Mrs. Claus	24,000+ backup reindeer
Dasher	Frosty the Snowman
Dancer	Sam the Snowman
Prancer	Yukon Cornelius
Vixen	The Abominable Snow Monster
Comet	A Wampa
Cupid	3 Dozen Tauntauns
Donner	The Spirit of Christmas Itself
Blitzen	

ELVES

Hermey the (Dentist) Elf	Weezy	Gabe
	Giggles	Plinko
GumDrop	Flinky	Hooha
Jingle	Bongo	Gerkin
Jangle	Zoinks	Puff
Don (formerly Lemonjello)	HappyPants (body not recovered)	Cinnamon
		Fungo
Ju-Jube	LaLa	Lumpkin
Fiddlepads	FaLaLa	Howdy
Chewbone	Hanky	Tinsel

Spike	Butterscotch	Tootsie
Benjable	Paragon	Major
Dim Sum	Omar	Powder
Spork	Maxwell	Crepe
Woofel	Whiskers	Zander
Flubber	Cabernet	Filibuster
Rider	Walt	Starburst
Cliff	Ben Ben	Lolly
B-Money	Janusz	Geza
Lupus	Soy	Kegel
Sprinkles	Ameer	Dallas
Jon Snow	LaDasha	Mistle
Sasquatch	Protein Bar	Friendship
Ayaan	Osama	O'Boo
Giant	Shakes	Bok Choy
Karen	Augustus	Bok Choy Jr.
Tinker	Peppy	Whisper
Hypertext	Claremorris	Gaggle
Adolf	Struwwelpeter	Lance Grover
Chachi	Aglet	Pettibone III
Sinphony	Whim	Woofers
Fennel	Pole Dance	Air Supply
Shakes	Major	Tinkles
Xanthe	Propecia	Skip
Hippocrit	Chumbawumba	Morrissey

ACKNOWLEDGMENTS

BRIAN SACK would like to thank:

My wives **Ewa** and **Karolina** for their support and mojitos, and a big bow to **the whole B.S. of A. gang** for being so talented and awesome.

JACK HELMUTH would like to thank:

The staff of The B.S. of A., who are pound-for-pound the most talented staff on television and exceeds expectations every week in putting on a show that normally requires four times the people.

Mike McDermott and **Ben Korman,** two of the aforementioned staffers, who helped with some of the photographs and graphics in this book on their own time. It's insane to me how talented these guys are.

Andrew Bowler, Brian Muchinksy, and everyone who helped me with the ideas and jokes contained in this book. Thank you for helping me walk the tightrope . . .

John Bobey for your constant guidance, support, creativity, and especially friendship. Thank you for getting me this job, which has changed my life in so many ways.

The staff at Burger Bistro in Park Slope, Brooklyn, where I wrote much of my portion of the book. Thank you for your patience and for letting me sit in your restaurant for days upon days while plying me with free Diet Coke refills.

Chris Balfe, Eric Pearce, and **Joel Cheatwood,** for this opportunity and especially for your patience and faith.

My family and friends who have collaborated with me, supported me, and loved me throughout the years. I can say with absolute certainty that I wouldn't be here without you. There are so many folks who I'm thinking of as I write this. My God I'm a lucky dude. I love you all so much.

And a very special thanks to **Betsy Helmuth**, who watched our two babies alone on the weekend as I went off to write this book. Betsy's patience, support, and encouragement was what allowed this book to happen. Thank you for everything you do for me and for our family. We're all so lucky to have you. I love you! More momma!

We would both like to thank:

Kevin Balfe, who edited this book in some of the meanest heated pools in America. Thank you for bringing this project to us and for trusting us with the idea. You made this happen, and we will always be grateful for that.

Glenn Beck, who came up with the original idea and allowed us to have it. Working for Glenn is a dream for a creative person, as he gives incredible freedom, trust, and latitude in the decisions he allows us to make. Beyond that, he is one of the nicest guys you could ever hope to meet. We are lucky to be able to call you both our boss and our friend.

Paul Nunn and the team of artists who did the artwork and graphics contained in this book. Open any page and you'll see just how talented these people are. Their hard work and patience with our long string of notes give this book a level of quality we didn›t dare dream of. Thank you so much.

Timothy Shaner put this book together in record time. Seriously, this book had no right to be published as quickly as it was, and that is due in large part to the talent and ferocity of Timothy. By the way, we have one more change . . . is it too late to include it?

Fans of the B.S. of A. who are fiercely loyal, smart, compassionate, and have great senses of humor. We make every decision on the show and now in this book with you in mind. You›re underserved in the laughter department and it is our objective to give you our best effort each and every day. Thank you so very much for your passionate support. We love you.

Book Stores for still selling books. Hang in there, fellas. We'll tell folks that there is a link between cancer and borrowing books from a library or something on our Twitter accounts.

Threshold Editions / Mercury Ink
A Division of Simon & Schuster, Inc.
1230 Avenue of the Americas
New York, NY 10020

First Threshold Editions/Mercury Ink paperback edition November 2013

THRESHOLD EDITIONS and colophon are trademarks of Simon & Schuster, Inc.

MERCURY INK is a trademark of Mercury Radio Arts, Inc.

For information about special discounts for bulk purchases, please contact
Simon & Schuster Special Sales at 1-866-506-1949 or business@simonandschuster.com.

The Simon & Schuster Speakers Bureau can bring authors to your live event.
For more information or to book an event, contact the Simon & Schuster Speakers
Bureau at 866-248-3049 or visit our website at www.simonspeakers.com.

Interior design by Timothy Shaner, nightanddaydesign.biz

Manufactured in the United States of America

10 9 8 7 6 5 4 3 2 1

ISBN 978-1-4767-6476-4
ISBN 978-1-4767-6477-1 (ebook)

Printed in the United States
By Bookmasters